To The Top

Reaching for America's 50 State Summits

NORTHWORD PRESS

Chanhassen, Minnesota

Text © 2003: Joe Glickman
Photography © 2003: Nels Akerlund,
except page 139: ©Dolly Alevizatos

Front cover: Mt. Rainier, Washington; back cover: Charles Mound, Illinois (left), Denali, Alaska (center), Black Mesa, Oklahoma (right); pgs. 4-5: Granite Peak, Montana; pg. 10: Mt. Whitney, California; pg. 40: Mt. Rainier, Washington; pg. 60: Mt. Katahdin, Maine; pg. 80: Brasstown Bald, Georgia; pg. 98: Mt. Arvon, Michigan; pg. 114: Mt. Rogers, Virginia; pg. 134: Denali, Alaska; pg. 140: Denali, Alaska

Edited by Barbara K. Harold
Designed by Russell S. Kuepper

NorthWord Press
18705 Lake Drive East
Chanhassen, MN 55317
1-800-328-3895
www.northwordpress.com

Library of Congress Cataloging-in-Publication Data

Glickman, Joe.
    To the top: reaching for America's 50 state summits / text by Joe Glickman ;
  photography by Nels Akerlund ; foreword by Jack Longacre.
        p. cm.
    Includes index.
    ISBN 1-55971-871-4 (hard)
      1. Mountaineering--United States--Guidebooks. 2. Hiking--United States--Guidebooks.
    3. United States--Guidebooks. I. Akerlund, Nels. II. Title.
GV199.4 .G55 2003
796.52'0973--dc21   2002032583

Printed in China

10 9 8 7 6 5 4 3 2 1

To The Top

Reaching for America's 50 State Summits

Text by Joe Glickman

Photography by Nels Akerlund

Foreword by Jack Longacre

Table of Contents

So, if you cannot understand that there is something in man which responds to the challenge of this mountain and goes out to meet it, that the struggle is the struggle of life itself upward and forever upward, then you won't see why we go. What we get from this adventure is just sheer joy. And joy is, after all, the end of life. We do not live to eat and make money. We eat and make money to enjoy life.

—Sir George Mallory

There are some that care not to listen but the disciples are drawn to the high alter with magnetic certainty, knowing that a great Prescence hovers over the ranges.

—Ansel Adams
Ansel Adams: An Autobiography

FOREWORD

YOU KNOW, it's really not a requirement that you be a mountain climber to read this book, although if you're not careful you may become one before you've finished it. If you already are a mountain climber—and especially if you are a highpointer—this book will provide much pleasure as you re-climb these mountains.

It's all here, the toughness and the solitude. From not knowing just where you're going, to finding your next "thank God" handhold on Granite Peak, to looking for a place to take a nap on Hoosier Hill.

The Highpointers Club holds an annual convention, often referred to as a "family reunion" (all right, mostly by myself). I get such joy from watching former rope teams hugging at these fiestas. When you rope up with someone on a serious mountain such as Rainier or Gannett, that rope becomes a connection that can last a lifetime. To stand by and watch old-timers telling their war stories is a joy to these old eyes.

I'm called the founder of the Highpointers Club, which may give the impression that the club was started on purpose and brought to the fore by myself. Not so. Arthur H. Marshall started highpointing way back in the 1930s. Arthur worked for the railroad and never learned to drive a car. He would get as close to his mountain as possible by rail, then hike, hitch, or hire a car and driver to take him to the trailhead. And I thought my highpoint days were rough! Sometimes he went through all that just to get to mountains like Casa Blanca and Massive in Colorado and Ocheydan in Iowa—which were considered highpoints at one time or another by the U.S.G.S. but turned out not to be. Oh well, Arthur thought he was on the right mountain, and he was, according to the cartographers and the club rules at the time.

Following Marshall was the well-known Stebbins Family. The father, C. Roland Stebbins, became the first person to do all forty-eight state high points twice when he re-climbed them with his sons.

Then Alaska and Hawaii became states, and all of a sudden there was a grand total of fifty highpoints to hit. The first to complete them was Vin Hoeman. Vin ushered in Frank Ashley, who wrote a small booklet on the fifty climbs. It was a guidebook in which I took much solace. I seriously question whether I could have mastered the highpoints without it.

Then and only then did I fall into the growing line of highpointers, and I've enjoyed every moment of it. As I said, I didn't start the club on purpose; it just sort of happened, happened, and happened. That story is pretty well covered in the Missouri chapter—I told it to Joe and Nels on our way up Taum Sauk—so I won't elaborate here.

Instead, I'll talk just a bit about this book. The writing is downright eloquent, presenting commonplace things in extraordinary ways. I especially appreciate phrases like "bionic lungs" and "acrophobic brain" that capture the humor in a difficult moment. And "more bogs than a Scotsman could shake a stick at" is just plain funny. There's a treat on every page as Joe Glickman masterfully guides his readers through the highs and lows of highpointing.

And what can I say of Nels Akerlund's exquisite photos? Eye-catchers, near every one—clever and thought-provoking, too. It takes some genius to capture the essence of snowy peaks and dusty hilltops alike, and Nels has done the trick.

The two of these young fellows epitomize all that is good about highpointing. To get to know them through their words and photos is to understand highpointing in its entirety. I have so much enjoyed reliving the fifty highpoints within this pictorial essay. Won't you join us?

Jack Longacre

Shortly before this book went to press, Jack Longacre died of cancer. He was 64. Three weeks before he died, he climbed Black Mesa in Oklahoma.

INTRODUCTION

YEARS AGO, a ski bum from Seattle told me that people fall into one of two categories: mountain people or ocean people. She spoke with such assurance I assumed the statement was true, and I've been trying to categorize myself ever since. In college I had befriended a hard-core mountaineer, and while I was working desk jobs in New York I'd get letters from him from Yosemite, Mexico, Peru, and Alaska. I got so much vicarious pleasure from his stories of climbing big walls and snowy peaks, I was sure I was a mountain person—although I hadn't done anything about it yet. Then in the early 1990s I discovered kayaking and began spending most of my free time paddling in Brooklyn's Jamaica Bay and in races in waters around the world. On paper, I looked like an ocean person.

In 1994 Nels Akerlund and I met during a month-long, 800-mile kayak race from Chicago to New York. A year earlier, Nels had paddled the Mississippi River solo. He had worked in Colorado on ski patrol and traveled alone through Alaska, South America, and Mexico. A professional photographer, Nels was ambitious, cocky and focused, and bristled with ideas about this river or that mountain. Two years after we met, he asked if I wanted to collaborate on a book about the Wisconsin River. I'd write it; he'd take the pictures. And so we did.

The night we finished, we were sitting in his house in Rockford, Illinois, feeling rather smug. Before I was halfway through my first beer, Nels announced that he wanted to do a book on the highpoint in each of the fifty states. "Are you in or out?" he asked. With an eight-month-old daughter on the scene, the thought of tackling a project that large thrilled me as much as hanging drywall in Madison Square Garden. "Not possible," I said. As Nels outlined his meticulous master plan—something about it taking only six months and making us lots of money—my latent fantasy of climbing big Western peaks, Alaska's Denali in particular, came bubbling to the surface.

A few months later, we met in Austin, Texas, and embarked on a month-long, ten-state, 2,500-mile road trip. That circuitous journey taught us some profound truths: First, on big, snowy mountains we had no bleepin' idea what we were doing. Second, while we knew we'd taken on a sizeable task, we'd underestimated how big (by a factor of ten as it turned out). We thought about abandoning the project. But those ten highpoints in the bag were an incentive to keep going. It was as if we'd invited a 500-pound gorilla to dinner that decided to stay for the summer.

Five years later, we were finished.

When we began, just fifty-eight people had climbed all fifty highpoints—typically more people climb Mount Everest in a single season. When we climbed Denali, our last highpoint, in July 2002, that number had risen to 110 and another 197 had hit all the highpoints in the Lower 48. While many of the highpoints are accessible to anyone with a car and the ability to put one foot in front of the other, standing on top of all fifty is surprisingly hard: You need time, money, and ample motivation (not to mention a good car stereo). If you're interested in doing something as ridiculous, difficult, but ultimately as satisfying as climbing highpoints, here are a few facts you may want to know:

To accomplish our goal, we drove approximately 12,000 miles and flew about as far again to Alaska and Hawaii. Because Nels was documenting our journey for this book, he shot 750 rolls of film for a cool $15,000. Tallying gas, motels, airfare, and food, we spent roughly $30,000. (Although a fair amount of that was spent in pursuit of the perfect latte.) Money aside, it's how much time passed between our first and last climb that seems so remarkable. During that time my mother died; my daughter, a babbling toddler when I left for Texas, learned to read. Nels got divorced and started a new relationship. Together we traveled to Thailand, Ecuador, and the British Virgin Islands to work on other stories. And the day before I was to fly to Chicago for highpoints in the Midwest, the World Trade Towers, less than two miles from my apartment in Brooklyn, were destroyed.

This collection of essays and photographs, as much a travel log as a book about highpoints, is a subjective version of what we saw, how we reacted and what we learned. Sure enough, Nels and I had our share of physical, emotional, and interpersonal discomfort. But as I write this, so close to the completion of our seemingly endless road trip, I feel thoroughly pleased that I let Nels talk me into doing something impractical, time-consuming and even, at times, dangerous.

Visiting high places, it seems, is an innate desire of our species. Whether it is the need to seek protection, perspective, or just space from people and machines, venturing where the air is colder, the wind stronger, the elements more ferocious, is as natural as seeking solace by the sea. And while many of the highpoints we visited weren't officially mountains, except for a handful, they all felt high. An important lesson in relativity.

Nels and I spent a night in the hulking stone tower on top of South Dakota's Harney Peak, a mountain the Lakota Chief Black Elk called "the center of the universe" (which, relative to the Lakota's world, it was). A plaque there informed us that all the moisture on the west side of the highpoint ran to the Pacific; all the run-off on the east side flowed to the Atlantic. Something about that captured my imagination. With a kick-ass pair of binoculars, could I stand up there and spy these two vast bodies of water? Probably not, but as the sun's bright red rays rose over a valley of improbably placed spires of granite, I imagined the water's inexorable journey from summit to sea.

From summit to sea; it's a lovely phrase. And the one leads to the other—in my psyche as well as in the physical world. Just as "high" is a relative term, the mountain/ocean dichotomy doesn't really exist either—you can't have the one without the other. Standing on the center of the universe, I made a mental note to tell my ski bum friend so when I returned. ▲

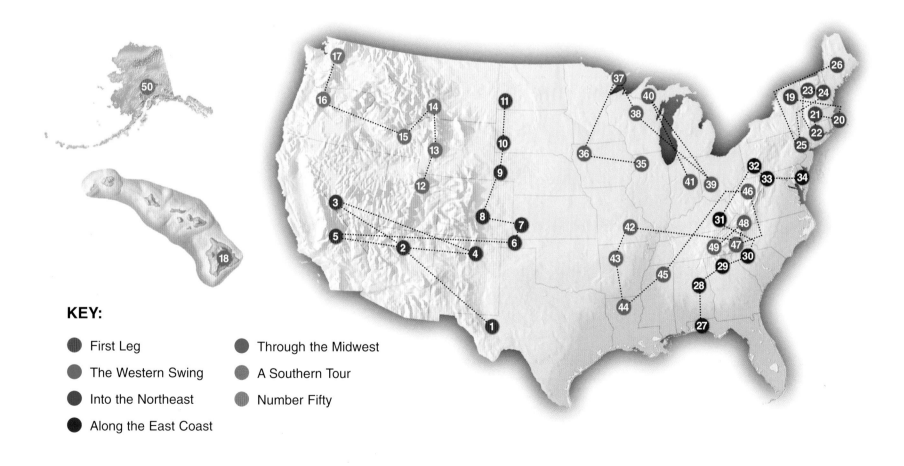

KEY:

🔴 First Leg

🔴 The Western Swing

🔴 Into the Northeast

⚫ Along the East Coast

🔴 Through the Midwest

🔴 A Southern Tour

🔴 Number Fifty

FIRST LEG

- Texas
- Arizona
- Nevada
- New Mexico
- California
- Oklahoma
- Kansas
- Colorado
- Nebraska
- South Dakota
- North Dakota

TEXAS Guadalupe Peak: *A Journey of 50 Peaks Starts with a Single Step*

First Leg

**Highest Elevation
8,749 feet**

NELS AND I MET in Austin and drove west through fields of wildflowers in the endless rolling hills of central Texas. At Van Horn, a small town with a big church that felt more Mexican than American, we headed north toward the Sierra Diablo Mountains. "No Gas for 100 miles," warned a sign on Highway 54 just before the pavement turned to red dirt. Creeping through a construction zone, we were waved on by a mud-splattered flagman, his face a mask of red. Perched along a ridge, three dozen white windmills spun against the gray sky like rotating crucifixes. The enormity of our project finally struck home: After we climbed Guadalupe Peak, we had forty-nine more highpoints to go.

As we turned into Guadalupe National Park, lightning slashed across an ominous-looking sky. Before you could say Don Diego de Vargas (the Spanish explorer credited with first seeing Guadalupe in 1692), rain pounded the car.

This had fun written all over it.

We sprinted from the car to the park's museum. It was closed. With nowhere to go and nothing to do, we stood under the eaves surveying the barren, wind-swept terrain that was once a stronghold of the Apaches and

their chief, Geronimo.

Guadalupe and her mate, El Cap, rise out of the Chihuahan Desert. To the early Spanish explorers, the bold outline of El Cap resembled a captain leading his men. In the late 1850s, the twin peaks were beacons for the stagecoach drivers on the Butterfield Overland Mail Route—a 2,700-mile journey from St. Louis to San Francisco. A hundred years later, early transcontinental airmail pilots also used the jagged peaks as a landmark.

A long, chilly hour later, the sky brightened, the wind died, and a breathtaking double rainbow appeared between the companion peaks. A park brochure, citing the wild weather swings—ice storms, vicious heat, and ferocious wind—in an area containing both desert and verdant canyons, dubbed the 86,000-acre National Park a "Land of Many Contrasts." To me it seemed more a case of multiple personalities.

At a campground at the base of the mountain, we dined on freeze-dried beef stroganoff under a full moon. Though it was April, we were at an elevation of about 5,800 feet, and the temperature dipped into the forties. Throughout the night, the wind roared like cars on a crowded freeway.

We had breakfast at the nearby Nickel Creek Cafe, a homey joint with religious artifacts and newspaper articles about rodeos covering the walls. It had been run for the past seventeen years by a fifty-year-old woman named Jo, who told us that some shingles had been blown off her house during the night. "It often reaches 100 miles an hour," she drawled. "Last night it was probably only around 70."

As we were getting ready to leave, a park ranger, the second customer of the day, ambled in. "Busy?" he asked.

"Sort of," she replied. Jo was so laid back I nearly felt compelled to check her pulse. Her stoicism and resilience were so unlike the hyper-urban New Yorkers of my hometown—so unlike me, actually.

Reading about the geological forces in the Visitor Center informed the way I looked at the stark terrain. Millions of years ago, the mountain range stretching south and east from neighboring New Mexico was a giant reef in a vast ocean. When the water vanished this limestone reef emerged, towering 4,000 feet above the desert. Halfway up the trail I found a fossilized seashell. Pretty good for my first hike on an ancient reef.

It took us just over two hours to hike the narrow, twisting trail to a primitive camp site 600 vertical feet from the summit. We set up our tent behind a low stone wall in a 40-mph wind. Thirty minutes later, we stood on the 8,749-foot summit. The view was grand—birds soaring on thermals, a desert that vanished into the horizon, a labyrinth of mountains and canyons dotted with stunted pines.

We returned to our tent to find a puffy purple-and-black sleeping bag laid out under a twisted hardwood tree. When I walked over to see if anyone was around, the bag bolted upright, holding a book on Aristotle. With the bag's

hood cinched around his unshaved face, the blue-eyed occupant looked like a cross between a monk and the Michelin Man.

His name was Mike. He was a rock climber and snowboarder who worked as a window washer in Telluride, Colorado, just long enough to fund his next vertical adventure. He'd spent most of the summer living in a cave in Yosemite, California, so that he could climb the famed big walls. For the time being, he was camped out in Hueco Tanks State Park, a hot climbing spot eighty miles away. Mike was young and smart and principled. Judging by the routes he'd tackled, he could climb his ass off.

As night enveloped us, the wind picked up and the temperature dropped. We talked about climbing and risk and death, and hard-core heroes like Yvon Chouinard and Royal Robbins until we were just three voices under a stark tree on a cold, windy mountain.

To me, Mike was plenty hard-core. He didn't let financial, emotional, or physical limitations stop him from realizing his adventures. He didn't appear reckless, but hunger, cold, even death were acceptable risks to him. David Brower, the founder of the Sierra Club, seemed to be talking about guys like Mike when he said, "You take risks. You search. Sometimes luck is with you, and sometimes not, but the important thing is to take the dare. A new fact has recently become clear to me: It is not variety that is the spice of life. Variety is the meat and potatoes. Risk is the spice of life. Those who climb mountains or raft rivers understand this."

Rain began to fall at 9 p.m. We retreated to our tent. Without a shelter, Mike seemed in for a long night. We burrowed into our sleeping bags and listened to the rain turn to hail as the wind howled overhead. I'd suffered through more than a few frigid nights outdoors, including a harrowing twenty-four hours in a blizzard in Montana during a kayak trip down the Missouri River. Nels had done his share of intense trips as well. But unlike Mike, we had careers, homes, and mates. Part of me admired people who pursued their dreams without a safety net. Another part craved comfort and routine—not to mention gourmet coffee. This quixotic trip we'd embarked on—from Alaska's Denali to Florida's Britton Hill—would merge significant risk and tame road-tripping.

At sunrise, I struggled with the frozen tent zipper to get out and relieve myself. The stark stone landscape was covered in ice. Mike was gone. Apparently he'd walked down during the night; no doubt headed to another mountain or elusive rock wall. Our next destination was Humphreys Peak in Arizona. Forty-nine highpoints to go. ▲

ARIZONA

Humphreys Peak: *Gee whiz!*

First Leg

**Highest Elevation
12,633 feet**

THE INCLINE HALFWAY UP the snowy slopes on Humphreys Peak was steeper than anything I'd previously stood on. I figured it was thirty-five degrees; Nels guessed fifty. (It was probably half that.) We had one ice axe between us and we'd both left our crampons in the car—a novice mistake made by two novices. No matter how steep the pitch, a slip would have sent us sliding down the slope like a teacup on a listing sailboat.

At 11,800 feet we reached the ridge that runs between Humphreys and its neighbor, Agassi, Arizona's second-highest peak. We saw a lone tent in a depression on the ridge. It was empty. We hunched behind some nearby rocks to get out of the wind. I gnawed on a frozen Power Bar, thinking about how we'd underestimated this mountain. The day before, in Flagstaff, we'd sat in shorts sipping coffee with a clear view of Agassi's inviting sun-drenched slopes. Today we huddled on an exposed ridge and hid from a biting wind.

The occupants of the tent arrived shortly, just back from the summit, and tossed their packs in the snow. The chattier of the two said he'd climbed Humphreys once a year for the past five years. When we mentioned we were

climbing highpoints, he lit a cigarette and told us about two friends who'd tried to climb Mt. Whitney. One, afflicted with altitude sickness, returned to camp; the other, an experienced hiker, continued up the mountain. He never returned. Apparently he fell through a cornice, slid 200 feet, and plunged off a cliff.

We were headed to Whitney in a week. Like Humphreys, the standard route up Whitney is not technical. Said simply, dying wasn't something we'd planned on doing on these long hikes.

We trudged on in the thin air, up a gently sloping ridge with a large overhanging cornice that led to the first of Humphreys' three false summits. The wind, 30 mph or more, shoved us toward the edge and an enormous snowy bowl far below. The billowy clouds that raced overhead cast huge, eerie shadows on the snow. According to the website maintained by the Highpointers Club, this 12,633-foot mountain in the San Francisco range is considered the easiest of the western highpoints (they rated it the tenth hardest overall).

But that provided little comfort as I moved along an exposed ridge thinking about the poor guy who'd fallen to his death on Whitney.

Perhaps we figured we could gloss over the holes in our climbing résumés. After all, we'd done our share of outdoor adventuring. Nels had paddled the Mississippi River solo; I'd done the same on the Missouri. I'd cycled across America; he'd hitched the length of Alaska, and we'd both competed in a thirty-day kayak marathon from Chicago to New York. And Nels had spent two seasons on ski patrol in Breckenridge, Colorado. Nevertheless, as mountaineers we had as much finesse as a couple of high-school kids sneaking into a singles bar.

In retrospect, our naiveté was comical. Two days earlier, approaching Flagstaff on a clear, sunny day, we debated if Humphreys would have any snow on it. Suddenly we crested a rise in the highway and—boom!—the hulking white form glared at us like the abominable snowman. Yet having seen the brilliant white slopes, the recipient of fifty inches of new snow, we didn't bring snowshoes or crampons. Sharing one ice axe was as efficient as eating soup with a fork. To add to our woes, the leather boots I'd recently purchased in New York rubbed my heels raw. I tried walking backward, which did ease the pain, but my progress was pitifully slow and I knew that if I ambled off a ledge I'd feel foolish.

An hour from the top, we were joined by a lanky Scotsman with a weathered face, ripped blue wool cap, corduroy pants, and thick wooden staff. He told us that there are 275 mountains over 3,000 feet in the Monroe Range back home and he'd climbed all but three. "If this mountain was in Scotland," he said in a lyrical brogue, "there'd be hundreds of people here." (We saw four.) He told us about his bum knee, said "Cheers," and left us far behind.

It took us six hours to cover the 4.5 miles, 3,500 vertical feet from the parking lot to the summit. The wind was 50 mph at the top. Below we studied the outline of the domed football stadium in Flagstaff; the white buttes, red rock, and rolling hills dotted with green pines; the faint line of the north rim of the Grand Canyon. I'd like to say that I spent my time in deep appreciation of our majestic surroundings, but in fact I was preoccupied with returning to the parking lot as soon as possible.

The walk up hurt my lungs; going down in the knee-deep snow damaged my blistered heels. Back at the car, I changed into dry clothes with all the energy of a dehydrated, blistered, famished, and sunburned wreck. I had so much dried gunk around my red nose that Nels dubbed me "Crusty."

I examined my ravaged feet while a carload of raucous teenagers partied in

the parking lot. Given my headache, their carefree laughter was galling. "Those kids have a lot of nerve," I said. Nels agreed, adding, "We could have died up there and nobody would have found us for days."

It was now apparent that the western highpoints that loomed ahead would exact a higher physical price than we'd thought. We'd had great weather on Humphreys, but the altitude, snow, and wind were more of a force than we'd banked on.

We were both thoroughly wasted but Nels, eager to get a jump on our next climb, wanted to push on to Las Vegas. By midnight we reached the Nevada state line. After all the solitude and darkness of the desert, I felt I was hallucinating as I negotiated the narrow road that slithers across the top of the well-lit, fortress-like walls of Hoover Dam.

Even stranger was Las Vegas, glimmering in the desert like the world's largest pinball machine. Had we not climbed a snow-covered peak that day, the scene would have merely been bizarre; given how addled we were with fatigue, it was Twilight Zone material. After just two mountains and a thousand miles of driving, it seemed our quirky road trip was only going to get stranger. ▲

NEVADA   Boundary Peak: *Death of a Salesman*

First Leg

**Highest Elevation
13,140 feet**

LAS VEGAS may be a neon city of sin, but to a pair of ravenous, low-budget mountain mutts the abundance of cheap breakfast buffets—designed to lure gamblers to slot machines—was simply divine. After a gluttonous all-you-can-eat feed, we drove into the desert with our bellies distended and our minds set on highpoint number three, Boundary Peak—at 13,140 feet, the tallest and most challenging mountain on our itinerary thus far.

As we headed north on Highway 264, the radio scanner spun endlessly in search of a station. Battered trailers with huge satellite dishes and littered front yards appeared on the arid horizon like prairie dogs popping up out of their holes. Dirt roads heading nowhere disappeared across scrub-brush plains. As the desert yielded to larger and larger mountains, we began to contemplate Boundary Peak long before we saw it. Would anyone else be there? How hard would it be? Which route should we take? Would we summit?

Outside of Dyer, Nevada, the town closest to Boundary Peak, we passed a sign that read "Dead Animal Pit." What the hell? Sure enough, it was a large open pit filled with decaying farm animals. In such a desolate setting, our stop at the pit felt uncomfortably portentous.

It took us a long time to find the dirt road leading to the mountain. Finally we found a white-haired farmer bumping along on a tractor. "There used to be a sign," he said flatly, "now there's just a post." Clearly, we could stop worrying about Boundary Peak being too touristy.

The twisted, rutted dirt road we crept along seemed to go nowhere forever. We bounced across dry streambeds, along crumbling ledges, over and around large rocks and up, up, up to an abandoned mine that seemed straight from a John Huston movie. The forsaken complex was eerie and beautiful; stark and lonely; a silent, dilapidated place with an aura of violence and desperation.

We stopped at the end of the 14.5-mile dirt road. The drive took an hour.

We set up camp at 9,600 feet near a rushing stream in a clearing littered with cow pies. It was Monday, April 28—the sixth day of our trip. According to the register at the trailhead no one had been here for two weeks. I would have thought two years.

As soon as the sun set, the cold settled around us. We built a fire and choked down some freeze-dried macaroni and cheese, a holdover from Nels' 1994 Mississippi River trip. It tasted like laundry detergent.

The wind shook our tent all night. If it was blowing this hard down here, what would it be like above 13,000 feet? The alarm rang at 5 a.m. but we lingered in our sleeping bags as long as possible. I don't know how Nels felt, but I didn't want to face the wind and cold in the dark.

At 6:30 we started down a soggy cattle trail through prickly brush and bristle pines, alongside a swift, narrow stream. By 8:00 we stood in a field and peered at the gnarly gray mountain for the first time.

Instead of hiking up the far ridge—the longer, gentler, more utilized route—we donned our crampons and headed straight up a ribbon of snow that led to the summit ridge. The footing was good but the slope was so steep I had to stop every twenty steps to catch my breath. Kicking steps into the snow inflamed the raw blisters I had acquired on Humphreys Peak.

At the top of the snowfield we found 700 feet of loose talus. We removed our crampons and scrambled up the sketchy slope that one climber likened to running uphill on marbles. When a rock the size of a garbage can bounded by, Nels said, "How about we do our next book on luxury swimming pools?"

On the ridge we had a clear view of the summit—or so we thought. We stowed our packs in the rocks and decided to dash to the top. As we got closer, the "real" summit appeared far above, beyond an outcropping of boulders three stories high that blocked our path. We inched our way along the right side, pressing against the icy rock like prowlers hiding from a searchlight. Beyond our toes was a 1,000-foot drop to the valley floor.

We were so tired we discussed heading down. But once we skirted the boulder field it was a straight shot to the top. By 12:30 we stood before a sea of snow-covered mountains. About a half-mile away in California, stood the slightly taller, far craggier, more menacing 13,441-foot Montgomery Peak. There was Mt. Dubois (13,559), White Mountain (14,246), and, farther west, the Sierras, including Mt. Whitney, the highest peak in the Lower 48.

I crouched out of the wind while Nels went to work. There was no sign of humanity; just mountains and sky. During our drive here from Las Vegas I had wondered why someone would live in the middle of nowhere. Now I flashed to a conversation I had had years ago with a craggy old codger at a cafe/bar/filling station in Baker, Nevada. He lived in the desert, fifty-six miles from the closest town. A classic crank, he complained bitterly about television (not the programming but the fact that it existed) and declared electricity the worst discovery in modern history.

"Why do you live so far from the highway?" I asked.

"To get away from the damned salesmen," he said matter-of-factly.

I laughed, pitying the door-to-door salesman who drew central Nevada for a beat. Ten years later, in a world so much more crowded and complicated by technology, his statement seemed far saner.

Above it all, on a timeless mountaintop, it occurred to me that people lived down barren dirt roads in Nevada for the same reasons most others stay away. Solitude. Heat. Space. The desert belongs to those who count its hardships among its blessings. For a few hours at least, I felt it belonged to me as well. ▲

NEW MEXICO

Wheeler Peak: *The Tube, Solitude, and Fast Food*

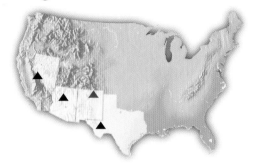

**Highest Elevation
13,161 feet**

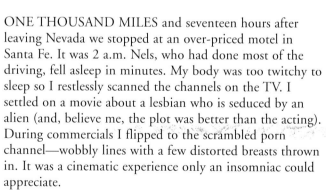

ONE THOUSAND MILES and seventeen hours after leaving Nevada we stopped at an over-priced motel in Santa Fe. It was 2 a.m. Nels, who had done most of the driving, fell asleep in minutes. My body was too twitchy to sleep so I restlessly scanned the channels on the TV. I settled on a movie about a lesbian who is seduced by an alien (and, believe me, the plot was better than the acting). During commercials I flipped to the scrambled porn channel—wobbly lines with a few distorted breasts thrown in. It was a cinematic experience only an insomniac could appreciate.

Much to my horror, the alarm rang at 8 a.m. Even after three cups of coffee, my eyes felt sandblasted. My desire to climb a steep 13,161-foot mountain was low, exceedingly low. And yet as we drove from Santa Fe to Taos I began to revive. Dramatic, liquid light bathed the pine trees climbing high up reddish-brown mountains; the adobe homes seemed part of the earth. Drive through New Mexico and you see why they call it "The Land of Enchantment."

Nels and I considered our two options for getting to the top: Bull-of-the-Woods, an eight-mile trail that rises 4,000 feet, and William's Lake, a three-mile trail that rises "just" 3,000 feet. While the William's Lake route is obviously shorter, the last mile gains 2,000 feet. In other words, it heads straight up the mountain. But fatigue or no fatigue, we'd arrived too late in the day to take Bull-of-the-Woods.

To access the William's Lake Trail, we drove up a twisting dirt road to the Twining Campground parking lot. Huge banks of snow ushered us onward. We parked in an empty lot near the Phoenix restaurant. We walked past a still chair lift at roughly 10,000 feet and followed cross-country ski tracks up a narrow trail through a stand of spruce.

There was an incredible amount of snow for May. We'd been wearing T-shirts down below and now we were walking in the waist-deep snow in snowshoes. I had been on this mountain before, but the scene bore little resemblance to my earlier visit. In 1990 I had biked from Portland, Oregon, east along the Columbia River to my uncle's house in Los Alamos, New Mexico—a thirty-one-day, 2,700-mile ride. After spending a few days with my uncle—a garrulous retired physicist—I was looking for something to do. I'd never hiked above 6,000 feet but climbing Wheeler suddenly seemed like a good idea.

It was a sunny day in July. Armed with a day pack and state road map, I headed up the trail feeling as if I were on a major expedition. Halfway to the top, I hooked up with a Hollywood stuntman, a muscular former Marine who regaled me with stories about jumping out of exploding buildings and burning cars (or was it burning buildings and exploding cars?). We walked hard in the thinning air, past scores of curious marmots, engaged in silent competition. Standing atop the summit, I felt quite macho—I'd hung with the Marine and made it over 13,000 feet—until a man and his five children joined us. The oldest was no more than eight; the dad had carried two of them.

On this snowy day in May, Nels and I faced a more challenging climb. We marched through the woods, often falling into pockets of snow that covered the tops of small pines, for two miles to William's Lake. The pristine lake I'd seen in the summer was now a solid, snow-covered depression at the bottom of a spectacular alpine bowl sparkling with ice. Save for the telemark ski tracks and avalanche trails on the backside of Taos, the neighboring mountain, the snow was unmarked. It glistened in the sun like a new plush carpet.

When we rounded William's Lake the grunt work began. The trail, which had turned steep, became steeper still, until our snowshoes slid down the slope. We lashed them to our packs and took turns kicking steps in the virgin snow. We zigzagged up the slope, sinking to our knees, and settled into an anaerobic, step-rest-step rhythm, stopping from necessity but using the opportunity to savor the view. This phenomenon—feeling like camel droppings while experiencing profound visual pleasure—was becoming familiar.

Two thousand feet above us was a ridge that led directly to the summit. To our right was an amphitheater of jagged rock, stunted evergreens, and snow. The wind was vicious on the ridge—50 mph or more. We leaned forward, focused intently on the huge cornice just to our left that hung like a frozen wave over a thousand feet of air. We trudged to the top, squinting like Mr. Magoo as ice particles lashed our faces.

It was 5:40 p.m. when we stood on top. I could feel my heart pounding in my chest. If we hurried we'd get back to the car before dark. "Let's get the hell out of here!" Nels yelled over the wind. Five minutes later we started

down. It was our shortest stay on a summit yet.

With the wind at our backs, we cruised down the steep slope, stumbling and laughing like a couple of teenagers—at least until I plunged the front fangs of my right crampon into my left calf.

We were back in Taos by 9 p.m. It was Sunday and we drove through the mostly deserted streets searching for an open restaurant.

By 9:30 we'd given up hope of finding real food and approached the counter at Burger King like a pair of ravenous cavemen with personality disorders. The meal was the culinary equivalent of the movie I'd seen the previous night, but when we'd slurped the last of the shakes and eaten our final fry, we sat back and basked in the glory of a day of sunshine, solitude, and snow. We were feeling rather, well, manly. Before I could get too pleased with myself, though, I had a vision of that father of five from ten summers ago, trudging toward the counter with his brood, covered in snow. ▲

CALIFORNIA
Mt. Whitney: *Big Mountain, Bigger Pancakes*

First Leg

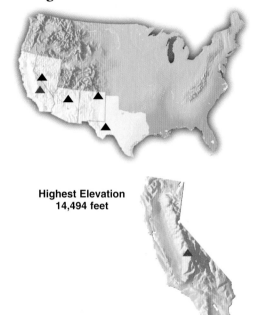

**Highest Elevation
14,494 feet**

AT 14,494 FEET, Mt. Whitney is the tallest mountain in the Lower 48 and the second-highest state point after Denali. This distinction, along with its beauty and proximity to Los Angeles and San Francisco, brings climbers in droves. For this reason, perhaps, I'd often heard the standard, walk-up route called "boring," "too crowded," and "too easy."

As someone who has graced the well-worn "cattle trail" with his size-thirteen hoofs, I'm here to say that Mt. Whitney is spectacular. Sure, there can be as many as 200 people on the mountain at any time—if you want seclusion, climb the technical east side—but the hiking mob I encountered did little to distract me from the waterfalls, lakes, streams, towering pine trees, snow-capped mountains, dramatic drop-offs, or towering walls of granite soaking up the sun's rays like chameleons basking in the window of an Ansel Adams exhibit.

I climbed Whitney a few years before Nels and I began our state highpoint project with my girlfriend (now wife) Beth. Nels climbed it in 1999 with his wife (now ex-wife). Beth and I were in Santa Barbara visiting her sister. We borrowed her sporty red Honda CRX and headed toward Death Valley. We secured a permit in Lone Pine and drove up the long, winding road into the Sierras with a mixture of excitement and nervousness. We'd cycled together across California, but never hiked for days in the wilderness and never above 10,000 feet. The thought of exceeding 14,000 was heady stuff. Park literature cautioned that it could snow any day of the year. Lightning storms are common in the summer. And without proper acclimatization, altitude sickness can strike hard and fast.

We heeded the 9,000 warnings not to leave any food in our car (bears!) and headed out along and over streams, through fragrant pine trees and below gray granite peaks. We spent our first night at Outpost Camp at 10,364 feet and spent the second night at Trail Camp. At 12,009 feet, this stark amphitheater is a chaotic collection of huge granite boulders. It overlooks Consultation Lake, a postcard-perfect lake with water cold enough to freeze your extremities—all of them—in seconds.

Morning dawned clear and cold. We made our way along nearly a hundred switchbacks to the famed John Muir Trail, which starts at Yosemite Valley and ends at Whitney's summit, 211 miles later. At Trail Crest (13,777 feet), the trail became exposed and offered mind-boggling views of the Sierras. We followed the narrow path to a jumbled field of boulders and then found our own way to the top of California—an endless, cruel, and beautiful landscape of jagged, gray peaks with patches of blue (lakes) and white (snow).

The scene up there was nearly surreal: people shouting to friends on their cell phone ("Guess where I am?"), hard-core climbers in helmets appearing over the east face, ultra-fit trail runners pausing on top before turning around on their one-day, twenty-two-mile jaunt, and scores of "regular" hikers.

We made it back to the Whitney Portal Store on the morning of our fourth day on the mountain. We'd mostly run out of food the night before and spent much of our time on the way down discussing what we planned to chow when we got back. The menu behind the counter announced that you could buy one, two, or three pancakes. "Eat three and they're free," said the sign.

Before ordering, I got into a discussion about mountaineering in the Sierras with the pony-tailed dude behind the counter. He'd skied up (and down) Whitney in the winter, and quickly dismissed me as cattle-trail material. (I was, but didn't like his attitude.)

I ordered the free stack, and the hipster said, "You won't finish 'em."

I'm six-feet-four and weigh 200 pounds. There are plenty of things I can't do—say, ski down Mt. Whitney—but eating a lot ain't one of them. "Yes, I will."

He seemed disgusted. "No one can."

"Bring 'em on, dude!" (Journalistic integrity compels me to report that I actually said "dude.")

We sat outside and waited, growing hungrier by the moment. Twenty minutes later, he appeared with three mutated, obscenely large pancakes— one-inch thick and large enough to be a hubcab on a tractor.

I was full long before I'd consumed the first. "Want one?" I asked Beth.

I walked around for a few minutes and had another go at the mound of dough. And still I couldn't finish one. I learned later that a professional cyclist, who'd ridden 100 miles with the sole mission of tackling the pancakes, was the only person to eat all three.

I waddled to the car feeling defeated. To add insult to injury, one window of our borrowed Honda had been smashed in by a bear that had sniffed out an unopened bag of popcorn we'd inadvertently left in the trunk.

We drove back to Santa Barbara with the wind racing through our crudely reupholstered car. When I stopped complaining about the size of the pancakes—"What's the point? What a waste!"—I realized that what bothered me even more than being categorized as a cattle-trail goof was the fact that I'd probably never get to know this magnificent country as well as the dude behind the counter at the Whitney Portal Store. ▲

OKLAHOMA

Black Mesa: *The Last Few Feet Are the Hardest*

Highest Elevation 4,973 feet

BLACK MESA, Oklahoma's 4,973-foot highpoint, a barren land of sagebrush, cactus, and tall grass, is a place of transition where the Rocky Mountains dissolve into the prairie; an area where species at the eastern- and western-most portions of their range meet. Cimarron County, which encompasses Black Mesa State Park, is the only county in America that borders four states—New Mexico, Texas, Colorado, and Kansas. (For the record, there are 3,070 counties in the U.S.)

We arrived in the dusty parking lot of Black Mesa State Park on a cool Monday afternoon in early May. After the vibrant, snow-covered mountains of New Mexico, the hardscrabble, mostly monotone country of the Oklahoma panhandle had a forlorn feel. According to the sign at the trailhead, this basalt-capped plateau, which rises 2,000 feet above the plains, was formed by the flow of an ancient volcano. The flat-topped mesa looks like the world's largest pool table. It's more than forty miles long, one of the largest mesas in the world.

The gentle, undulating jeep trail winds its way through cactus, lava rock, stunted junipers, and prickly bushes to the side of the chiseled, crumbling talus slopes of the giant mesa. The arid landscape begins to make more sense when you learn that the temperature ranges from –30°F to 112°F, and that the area receives less than fourteeen inches of annual rainfall.

In the distance was a lone homestead; the kind of place you'd expect to stumble across in a John Wayne western. Given its no-man's-land feel, it was no surprise that just four miles away was a haunt called Robber's Roost, a haven for outlaws who specialized in rustling cattle, horses, and sheep.

The trail zigzags up a rocky, crumbling cliff to the top of the mesa. This short, steep section gains 700 feet over roughly half a mile. On top it's as if you've entered a different world. Suddenly the desert-like landscape is transformed into a flat, seemingly endless field with a smattering of dwarfed vegetation resembling Homer Simpson's hair.

We walked south and west for about three miles on the flat trail to a nine-foot granite monument standing smack in the middle of an eighty-acre tract that seemed no higher than anything we could see for miles. Nels sighed. "How am I going to photograph this sucker? It looks like an empty field!"

We milled around the monument like two guys waiting for a bus. The four faces of the monument pointed out the distances to significant landmarks: East: Kansas, 53 miles. West: New Mexico, 1,299 feet. North: Colorado, 4.7 miles. South: Texas, 31 miles. It was 895 miles to Los Angeles and 1,605 miles to my home in New York City.

I sat on the chilly concrete base, reclined against the slick monument and began reading the logbook. Donna Duerr, who said she was the second woman to climb all fifty highpoints, wrote, "Nice monument; easier than Denali." A guy from Nashville waxed philosophical, "Don't wrestle with a pig. It makes you dirty and annoys the pig." And a woman from Tulsa wrote, "What a place to conceive my next child."

We walked to the edge of the mesa and gazed west at New Mexico's volcanic mountains. Nels' essential dilemma persisted. "What the hell do I shoot here?" He shot me leaning up against the monument in every which way and still he wasn't satisfied. Finally, after more than an hour he asked, "Could you climb up on the monument?"

The request was reasonable enough; I just wasn't sure how I was going to haul my lanky carcass up there. The upward-angling sides were as slick as, well, polished granite. The top, nine feet above the concrete base, was less than two feet across. While I don't consider myself particularly afraid of heights, I eyed the modest top the way a non-swimmer would a pool without a lifeguard.

I put my foot into Nels' clenched hands, stepped up, grabbed the far edge and pulled myself into a sitting position on top. Nels set up his tripod and took a bunch of shots. He shouted, "Could you stand up?"

My heart beat erratically. My backside was practically hanging off the edges. How could I stand up on this tiny square without falling? Nine feet doesn't sound very high, and it's not really, but my suddenly acrophobic brain calculated that it was high enough to render me a paraplegic.

I've gone hang-gliding and climbed rock and ice faces hundreds of feet high. I even jumped nude off a fifty-foot cliff off the coast of Yugoslavia. Still I was only slightly more mobile than the monument. Nels, who's done far more rock climbing than I, treated me with kid gloves: "Just stand up!"

"I can't!"

"How come?"

"I dunno!"

It was absurd, but I couldn't get my brain to budge my feet.

After nearly fifteen minutes, I slid down, as embarrassed as a man retreating down the ladder on the high dive.

I gave Nels a boost and, before you could say Cimarron River Valley, he popped up into a standing position, as comfortable as a steelworker on a girder.

I took a few shots of him standing atop this elongated podium as the sun set behind him. A silly photo opportunity at the end of a mellow day had been as trying as any situation I'd yet encountered in the mountains. ▲

KANSAS Mt. Sunflower: *Feeling Lofty Down Low*

First Leg

**Highest Elevation
4,039 feet**

WHILE I'M NOT HERE TO DEBUNK the romance of life on the road, I should mention that climbing highpoints, especially out West, involves copious amounts of car time. The drive from Black Mesa, the highpoint in Oklahoma, to western Kansas was long and tedious. The barren terrain and darkness that gradually enveloped us magnified our fatigue. At 2 a.m. we tossed our sleeping bags on the cold concrete floor of a dreary roadside pavilion in Weskan, Kansas—more a wide spot in the road than a town.

The wind, the drone of the grain elevators across the street, and the glare of the overhead lights made sleep difficult. At first light we woke feeling stiff, groggy, and hungry. Nels, his hair spiked skyward in a terminal case of sleeping-bag head, said groggily, "I got up on the wrong side of the concrete this morning."

But then he looked up at the sky and leapt up. "The light is perfect. Let's go!" Before you could say "Auntie Em" we were speeding north down a two-lane country road as straight as a corn row en route to the highpoint of the Sunflower State.

After two weeks of climbing in Texas, Arizona, Nevada, and New Mexico we were still under the spell of the Southwest: big mountains, dramatic scenery, magical light—home to artists like Georgia O'Keefe, dedicated ski bums, and spiritual seekers. Call me a pessimist, but I expected Mt. Sunflower, our first highpoint of the Great Plains, to be about as exciting as the weather channel.

But Sunflower shone on two fronts: Not only was it interesting, it was amusing. After making a hard left onto a gently undulating dirt road, we came to a Dead End sign next to a brightly painted wood cutout of a jagged, snow-covered mountain, with an arrow pointing to the foreboding peak.

We parked twenty yards from the "summit" and ambled the last few feet to an eclectic monument constructed on privately owned farmland 4,039 feet above sea level. Technically, a mountain must have a 2,000-foot difference in altitude from summit to base in a ten-mile radius, so the "Mt." in Mt. Sunflower was a misnomer. Nevertheless, on this gentle mound of farmland, a mere jog from the Colorado state line, we stood higher than anyone in the state of Kansas.

We circled the monument: a ten-foot, fenced-off square filled with a funky collection of incongruous…stuff. A tall sunflower (*Helianthus annuus*, the state flower) built out of railroad spikes was the centerpiece. Next to it was a towering bare tree trunk—so sun-bleached it was as white as a chicken bone— with a cow's skull perched atop. Also included was a rain gauge (nearly empty) and large tumbleweeds pinned by the wind against the wire fence surrounding the monument. A stone plaque read, "In loving memory of Edward and Elizabeth Harold. Homesteaders, 1906."

While Nels continued shooting, I sat at a nearby picnic table and read the summit register that was housed in a bullet-riddled mailbox mounted to a fence post to the right of the sunflower. "Congratulations!" it read in bold letters. "You have conquered Mt. Sunflower…The west and north approaches to the mountain are attainable only by native cattle traffic…Local nature guides are available at tremendous expense."

To the west, the Great Plains climbed to merge with the foothills of the snowy Rockies, which I had at first confused with the large, puffy clouds hovering in the distance. (Ian Frazier, author of *The Great Plains*, said of the sky that touches the horizon, "The sky is like a person yawned and never stopped.") Behind me, the plains descended to the river valleys, some of the most fertile land in the country.

It was a lonely, quiet place, and somehow this homespun collection of manmade and natural objects captured the spirit of those who were able to endure, even prosper, in a harsh, powerful land.

Less than a mile away to the northeast, in a low grove of trees, was the Harold homestead. Land that had been watered was as green as a golf course; elsewhere it was dry and barren. Listening to the whinny of a horse on this chilly morning in May it was easy to imagine what life had been like at the turn of the century when the first Harolds settled here a few decades after the last battles between whites and Indians. The buffalo were gone, but the wind, which whistled in excess of 30 mph, remained a dominant presence—persistent, eternal.

In the register, the Harold family had written that visitors should feel free to stop by the house to tell them about "your trials and tribulations on your way to the lofty height." We considered stopping by but didn't. Everything about Mt. Sunflower had been a pleasant surprise—even this invitation—and we figured we wouldn't press our luck. We got back in the car and headed west to the Rockies, where the snow-covered mountains are far more spectacular, but not nearly as cordial. ▲

COLORADO Mt. Elbert: *Hopeless or Ropeless?*

**Highest Elevation
14,433 feet**

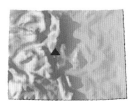

AFTER TWO WEEKS ON THE ROAD Nels and I weren't exactly sick of each other but we were getting close. We squabbled about money and conducted socio-political debates on chain stores and fast food. (At the time Nels still enjoyed the occasional Whopper. I eventually converted him, but that's a story for another mountain.) After 336 continuous hours side-by-side in a car or tent, or on a chilly mountain, the differences in our personalities, which typically complemented each other, were grating on our respective nerves.

We needed a break from each other. Instead, we went to Leadville, Colorado, to climb Mt. Elbert, highpoint number seven.

Once the West's wildest and richest silver mining boomtown, 30,000 strong, Leadville was famous for violent labor conflicts and flamboyant characters like Doc Holliday, Kit Carson, and Buffalo Bill Cody, who passed through at the end of the nineteenth century. Today this quaint, quiet town of 2,600 at the headwaters of the Arkansas River is seventy square blocks of Victorian architecture adjacent to a twenty-square-mile mining graveyard. Located in a high mountain valley at 10,430 feet, Leadville is the highest incorporated city in North America.

Mt. Elbert is the king of the Rockies, the tallest peak in a state with fifteen mountains higher than 14,000 feet. Despite its lofty status, no one in town seemed to pay it much attention. The chain-smoking woman at the bookstore, whom we interrupted in a heated conversation about guns (". . . the son of a bitch shot off his finger," she said), had virtually no literature on the mountain. The woman at the Chamber of Commerce was equally uninformed. In fact, no one I asked, including the hip, pony-tailed dude at the outdoor shop who'd climbed the 14,433-footer a few times, knew why the second-highest mountain in the Lower 48 was named Elbert. Only after I returned home and reconnected with the all-knowing Internet did I get the inside scoop.

Samuel Hitt Elbert (1833-1899) became Governor of Colorado in 1873 when the state was still a Territory. His appointment coincided with the discovery of gold and silver in the San Juans, which were then part of the Ute reservation where mining was forbidden. Elbert, who had his own mining interests in the area, pushed some political buttons and before you could say "Eureka!" the Utes were plumb out of luck. The move so thrilled some prospectors that they inscribed "ELBERT PEAK" in the soft metal of a shiny tin plate and placed it on the summit. Later that summer, Henry W. Stuckle, a member of the surveying party credited with the first climb, found it. While the name Elbert does not invoke the majesty of the highest peak in the Rocky Mountains, it's probably better than Mt. Stuckle.

At 7:30 a.m. we parked at 10,000 feet and started up a muddy, dirt road in light snow. The road led to a narrow, snowy trail through a dense grove of bare aspen, which grew shorter and more spindly as we went. When the snow got too deep we donned our snowshoes and trudged on for two sweaty hours up the steep, serpentine trail before we emerged above tree line.

In another two hours we were on the huge, exposed side of Elbert. From there it seemed a straight shot to the top. We stowed our snowshoes behind some rocks, strapped on our crampons, and continued up on the hard-packed snow. It was a perfect day: blue skies, no wind, with temperatures in the thirties. There was not another soul in sight. Still, the altitude hurt, especially when one of us sank into a thigh-high snowdrift.

Each time we thought we were near the top, we'd spy another rounded false summit far above. It was as one guidebook said, "You will appreciate Elbert's size long before you reach the summit." Far below, Twin Lakes, a pair of beautiful long lakes half-covered by ice, glimmered in the distance.

Half an hour from the summit, Nels announced that we should go left on the broad snow slope. I didn't like the tone of his voice and went right. I thought I heard him mutter, "You're hopeless." We'd been walking for five hours, in silence. I was tired, hungry, and now furious.

I'd been breaking trail all day and I decided that I was going to teach him a lesson and race to the top alone. Ten minutes later, I slowed like a turtle on Valium. Nels caught me after a few minutes and we walked sullenly side-by-side the rest of the way.

There's something about standing on top of a big mountain to change your attitude. With a 360-degree view of a sea of snow-capped giants—the Sawatch, Mosquito, Sangre de Cristo, and Elk ranges—stewing over a petty insult suddenly seemed…petty. We were the first hikers to sign the summit register in nineteen days.

At 1:45 p.m., clouds descended around us, the wind picked up and snow fell hard. We had spent only twenty minutes on top, but our footprints were gone. The wind raked across the mountain so hard that the left side of my face became painfully cold. Finding our snowshoes in this white blur would not be easy.

Twice Nels led us astray. As we wandered around in a snowstorm, especially when we had to walk back uphill, my resentment resurfaced. We searched where we thought we'd left the snowshoes, making tighter and tighter circles like a country dog looking for the best spot on a rug. Finally, mercifully, there they were, nearly buried in the snow. Even wearing them we sank in up to our knees. Had we not found them we'd have had one brutal walk down in the dark.

The climb had taken ten hours.

I sat in the car next to Nels, so drained I could barely remove my wet leather boots. Nels was tired too but he seemed thoroughly content. Didn't he notice how angry I'd been? I told him I'd been offended by his insult.

He seemed confused.

"You called me hopeless!" I said.

He offered another baffled look. I lost confidence.

"What about clueless?" I asked.

He looked indignant. "I said 'ropeless!' It's dangerous to be ropeless on such a steep slope."

Ropeless, hopeless, clueless, or snowshoeless? I didn't believe him, but I admired his quick reply and appreciated his tact. Because, of course, it didn't really matter. Together, we'd climbed our highest peak yet and managed a potentially difficult descent in a whiteout.

Back in Leadville, we laid waste to two huge bowls of chili and double-scoop ice cream cones. Stuffed and satisfied, we got back in the car and headed out to climb another mountain. ▲

NEBRASKA
Panorama Point: *Watch Your Step*

**Highest Elevation
5,424 feet**

PERCEPTION IS OFTEN FRAMED by what came before. A day earlier, we had leaned into the wind in a snowstorm on 14,433-foot Mt. Elbert in Colorado. By contrast, the charms of Panorama Point, a bump on a gently rolling stretch of farmland, seemed exceptionally tame. It was mid-afternoon, and we stood next to a small gray stone monument in the middle of a field of bleached bones and cow pies. But my mind's eye was still full of views of the snow-capped Rockies. The reality of the deserted field in the southwestern corner of the Nebraska panhandle made me want to take a nap.

At 5,424 feet, Nebraska's highpoint was roughly 5,000 feet below our starting point on Elbert. This peak-to-plains contrast—as dramatic as between any two highpoints we would visit back-to-back—underscored the quirkiness of our not-always-lofty pursuit. Unlike those who climb the fifty "best" mountains in America, dedicated highpointers explore out-of-the-way places they'd probably never otherwise see.

Panorama Point is such a place. Finding the windswept spot where three states converge was more of an exercise in location scouting than in

mountaineering, or even hiking.

After a night at the Stage Coach Inn in Cheyenne, Wyoming (at $22.98 for a double, a veritable steal), we headed east along I-80 toward Nebraska. We sped past vast tracts of flat, treeless land covered in tall grass. When we turned off the highway at the small town of Pine Bluff, Nels stated the obvious, "Not the kind of place you'd build a ski chalet."

We attempted to follow the guidebook's directions through a maze of county roads—164, 203, 1, 6, and 5, to be precise. Eventually we found our way down a rutted dirt road past a windmill that led to the weathered white stone monument marking the confluence of Wyoming, Colorado, and Nebraska. Erected in 1869, the marker was inscribed only with "Colorado," the Territory in which it then stood. A new base with the three state names was built in 1981.

If you stand at the tri-state marker, squint, and know where to look, the highpoint marker in the distance is just barely visible. (The exact spot wasn't "discovered" until 1951.) We drove a bit farther, parked by a bunch of scattered planks from an old wagon that had been bleached white by the sun, and walked up a gentle rise in a stiff wind.

Standing all alone was a four-foot-high gray granite obelisk on a concrete base surrounded by a knee-high fence that quite possibly could have deterred a toddler from molesting the monument. Adding to the understated weirdness of it all was a battered, gray metal drafting table that stood a few feet to the side.

We milled around the monument like a couple of guys looking for a street address we couldn't remember. Nels hurled a flattened cow pie downwind like a Frisbee. I opened the metal desk and copied inscriptions from the logbook until my pen ran out of ink.

The majestic Rockies shone 100 miles to the southwest. A half-dozen grain silos stood to the west, presumably belonging to the Constables, who still owned the land (for years, the highpoint was called Constable Point). The fluttering sound of flying grasshoppers and the twitter of birds were nearly drowned out by the wind ripping across the plains. The monochromatic flatness left us, charged with documenting the spot, with two choices—to look more closely and discover the subtle layers of detail, or to take a nap.

Nels seemed stymied. "This is *really* uneventful. How do I capture a field of

wind that happens to be the highest point in the state?" I offered a few suggestions. There was the gray metal table and headstone, the brown metal railings speckled with white bird droppings, a sea of brown-and-white cow pies, grass bleached white, green fields, and big fluffy clouds in a huge blue sky. He seemed unimpressed. "The big event on this climb was when your pen ran out of ink. Perhaps you could pose by the metal desk with the pencil you found."

Nels couldn't seem to accept that although we stood on the twentieth tallest highpoint in America, a place higher than downtown Denver, we were in an endless, empty field, in hardscrabble country that novelist Willa Cather described in *My Antonia* as "grey as sheet-iron." I thought of avant-garde composer John Cage, who once said that if he ever found a noise ugly, he kept listening until it sounded beautiful.

I lay down in a grassy patch, facing the sun. Save for the antelope that flashed by, nothing happened. It was peaceful. I imagined that the settlers who endured four seasons of dust and heat, relentless wind and brutal winters, would appreciate an afternoon like this.

When I woke up, Nels was sprawled on the ground like a rifleman taking cover—only he was hunkered behind multiple mounds of artfully arranged cow poop rising out of the plains like foothills. He was clearly enjoying himself. So we weren't 14,433 feet up in the Rockies. We had each found a way to experience the essence of this out-of-the-way spot where highpointers come to roost and cows come to unburden themselves. ▲

SOUTH DAKOTA

Harney Peak: *The Center of the Universe*

First Leg

**Highest Elevation
7,242 feet**

I THOUGHT I KNEW what South Dakota looked like. After all, I had paddled down the middle of it on the Missouri River in 1995. To me, South Dakota was the lifeless rolling hills of the Badlands and treeless prairie I passed through during my seventy-seven-day paddle from Montana to New York.

The Black Hills National Forest—a relatively small, forested oasis with a look and feel all its own—took me completely by surprise.

Harney Peak sits in the southwest corner of the state among a jumbled collection of wild granite spires and dark green ponderosa pines that appear nearly black from a distance. The Lakota Sioux called this area Paha Sapa, or "hills that are black."

The spectacular needle-like formations inspire a feeling of reverence, even awe. The Sioux considered this geographical anomaly a holy wilderness, and early white explorers dubbed a 6,800-foot formation Cathedral Spires. Having just spent half the day in a barren field of cow turds on Nebraska's Panorama Point, Nels and I felt transported, nearly giddy. "Rock makes a park!" he said as we drove up the winding two-lane road into Custer State Park.

We arrived at the lodge overlooking Sylvan Lake late in the afternoon. On the wide wood deck, I met Tom, a retired cop in full cowboy garb, who had left the Miami Police Force after twenty-three years. "This is my place," he said. He was a proverbial walking encyclopedia about Harney Peak. He told me that General George Custer, the West Point grad who rarely met an Indian he didn't want to kill, attempted to climb Harney in 1874. "They stumbled down in the dark," he said. "In one place the men supposedly had to hold the horses' tails for footing."

The first white to summit, he said, was an army surgeon, Dr. Valentine T. McGillycuddy, who stood atop in 1875. (The doctor, said to be the white man who knew Crazy Horse best, had his ashes placed in the tower's stone stairway.)

Tom said that the lookout on top, a fire tower until 1967, was built by the Civilian Conservation Corps and completed in 1939. "They've had weddings up there," he said proudly.

With ninety minutes of daylight left and three miles to the summit, we rounded Sylvan Lake and hustled up the well-worn, snowy dirt trail canopied by stands of pines. Twice we stopped to watch deer wander by. Wary of losing the trail in the dark, we walked with purpose and made it up just before sunset.

An impressive stone structure sat like a fortress atop the mountain. We climbed the stairs to the open garret—maybe thirty feet above the ground—unrolled our sleeping bags and donned all the warm clothing in our packs. A sliver of moon graced the sky. To the east and south the lights of a town glimmered below. A sign said that the 7,242-foot Harney Peak was the highest point east of the Rockies and west of the Pyrenees in Europe. Since no one else was around, that meant we were the highest humans east of the Rockies and west of the Pyrenees.

Between us we had a bag of trail mix, a box of fig cookies, water, and a bottle of tequila. Dinner didn't last long so we broke out the booze. As the contents of the bottle dwindled, the wind intensified. Buried in our sleeping bags against the thick, cold stone wall, we launched into a discussion of the weighty subjects drunk men discuss on mountains—women, food, and back to women—until we drifted off to sleep.

At 5:30 a.m. I was awakened by a wailing voice in the distance. I glanced over at Nels; he was gone. Listening more closely, I heard Nels shouting over the wind. "It's beautifulllllll!" he called in an annoying, high-pitched voice. I tried to ignore him but he wouldn't shut up. "It's beautifulllllll!" he cried again and again, like a eunuch in a wind tunnel.

Irritated, I exited my bag into the cold morning feeling tired, sore, and hung over. However, the moment I scanned the horizon—boom!—I felt the power of the place. The first rays of light lit the far distance and the shadowy, needle-like granite spires peaked above the low wispy fog. The sky was filled with stars. I replied in an operatic voice only a hearing-impaired mother could love. "It's beautifulllllll!"

It was one of the most magical scenes I've ever awoken to. I walked around the summit as the sun climbed over the surrounding hills. I had a panoramic view of South Dakota, Nebraska, Wyoming, and Montana. I felt a surge of energy and sense of well being that has to be experienced to be understood. I learned later that Black Elk, an Ogallala Sioux medicine man, who lived in the late-1800s, called the South Dakota highpoint "the center of the universe." In fact, in the world before air travel he was largely correct—Harney Peak is not far from the precise geographical center of the United States. Black Elk first visited the summit when he was nine years old and returned many times for vision quests and spiritual rejuvenation.

Here is his description of standing on the highpoint, from the book, *Black*

Elk Speaks:

"Then I was standing on the highest mountain of them all, and round about beneath me was the whole hoop of the world. And while I stood there I saw more than I can tell and I understood more than I saw. For I was seeing in a sacred manner the shapes of all things in the spirit and the shape of all shapes as they must live together like one being. And I saw that the sacred hoop of my people was one of many hoops that made one circle, wide as daylight and as starlight, and in the center grew one mighty flowering tree to shelter all the children of one mother and one father. And I saw that it was holy."

You may think these are the words of a mystic, that only a Native American could tap into the energy of nature so intensely. But visit the summit of Harney Peak. Spend the night if you can. Watch the sun rise. Even if the poetry of Black Elk's words is denied you, you may find yourself shouting, "It's beautifulllllll!" And that will be good enough. ▲

NORTH DAKOTA

White Butte: *Hay Waits For No Man*

First Leg

**Highest Elevation
3,506 feet**

THE ANIMATED VOICE on the radio commercial said, "Hay waits for no man!" Goofiness aside, the slogan seemed to speak volumes about the harsh weather and hardscrabble farm country we sped through. We were headed north from South Dakota to White Butte on the North Dakota–Montana border.

Located seven miles southeast of Amidon (population 40), White Butte resides in Slope County (population 767), an area larger than Rhode Island that enjoys the distinction of being the least-populated county in the state. That's saying something: North Dakota has just 690,000 people within its borders, and most of them live in the flat, fertile region to the east. The grassland to the west is ranch country, an area so desolate that when we passed another car, Nels took to lifting a finger off the steering wheel to acknowledge the other driver's presence. He didn't have to lift often.

We turned off Highway 85 onto a gravel road, drove for 3.9 miles, turned onto another straight road that looked exactly the same, continued for 10.6 miles, turned onto another straight dirt road for 5.5 miles and pulled up to a weather-beaten farmhouse with the name Buzalsky barely visible on the mailbox. If Slope County is the sleepiest county in North Dakota, we were in the narcoleptic part of Slope County.

We loitered by the car for a few minutes, feeling anxious about being on private property. A stiff wind muted the sounds of nearby cows, pigs, and sheep. A few moments later, a big guy with a week-old beard, gray flannel shirt, and baseball cap with a warped brim ambled out of the house, a puppy bouncing along by his side. He could have used a stout pair of suspenders.

As it turned out, Frank Buzalsky was an affable fellow who spoke in short, straightforward sentences. He told us that his great-grandfather, who'd moved here from Minnesota around the turn of the century, spent as much time making moonshine as he did farming. "I remember the bullet holes in his car," he said. We talked about the weather (they'd had twenty-eight inches of snow and 70 mph winds on April Fool's Day), about his son, who raised hunting dogs, and about trying to make a living in southern North Dakota. As he spoke, I kept thinking how tough you had to be to live out here. It was May 9—spring just about everywhere else—and it was 15°F without the windchill. And it was windy. I was cold in my down coat. Frank seemed comfortable in just a flannel shirt.

Given the incessant wind, long, brutal winters, and lack of company, one can see why moonshine was once a popular local brew. In the old days, before MTV and the Internet, it wasn't uncommon for a man who'd had to leave home for a few weeks to return to find his mate suffering from anemomania, or wind madness. Despite the hardships, Frank said, "I wouldn't live anywhere else."

Though you must skirt four barbwire fences and (in warm weather) be wary of the rattlesnakes, it's a pleasant one-mile hike up a cattle trail to the top of White Butte. After seventeen days on the road, this was to be our tenth and last highpoint on the first of many road trips. The thought of heading home, and the excitement of being in such an isolated place—"Not even the locals know about White Butte," Frank had said—inspired me to run spontaneously to the top.

Standing atop the 3,506-foot rise it's easy to see where it got its name: There's plenty of white rock and soil in the surrounding buttes. The mud puddles were chalky; even the grasshoppers were white. There was a metal stake shaped like a mushroom that marked the top and a memorial to Lawrence P. Buzalsky (1935-1990). Frank had said that we were about the twentieth visitor in the past five months. According to the summit register, though, we were the thirteenth in the last two years.

The simplicity of the land is part of its power. My two-year-old daughter could have drawn the landscape. On the bottom of the page she'd have colored in the neutral hills and eroded buttes; on the top, blue sky and puffy white clouds. Somewhere below us were old Indian burial grounds as well as more Tyrannosaurus Rex bones than any place on Earth. Nearby, Sitting Bull was shot in the hip in a skirmish with soldiers in 1864. On his ranch in Medora, forty-five miles north, Teddy Roosevelt escaped the crowds back East to recover from the near-simultaneous deaths of his first wife and mother.

I stood there awhile, gazing out at the empty, harsh, timeless landscape. Save for the changes caused by the wind, rain, and snow, this stark place probably looked much the same 25,000 years ago. It was a peaceful final resting place for man and beast alike. But the feeling on White Butte wasn't mournful; rather, it was a contemplative place with a healthy dose of grandness; a place that forces you to face silence and confront your true nature. Teddy Roosevelt said it best, "We are so rarely able to actually, and in real life, dwell in our hero land." ▲

THE WESTERN SWING

- Utah
- Wyoming
- Montana
- Idaho
- Oregon
- Washington
- Hawaii

UTAH   Kings Peak: *Bugs, Sweat, and Tears*

**Highest Elevation
13,528 feet**

COMPARED TO THE DESERTED TRAILS we had encountered on our first trip out West the previous spring, the trailhead to Kings Peak was bustling. As we sorted our gear on a sunny July 4th weekend, we chatted with a Forest Ranger who was heading into the hills with a pack llama. We exchanged cool-guy-isms with two hip snowboarders from Salt Lake City. And we bantered with a woman who was hiking in sandals because she'd recently dropped a computer (a laptop, fortunately) on her toes.

Minutes later, two moose moseyed by. It was a smorgasbord of activity.

Four days earlier, I'd driven from Brooklyn to Nels' home in Rockford, Illinois. We threw our gear into his green Jeep and cruised through the Midwest into Wyoming, where the West really starts to feel like the West. In Laramie, we stopped at the Purple Dragon Tattoo Parlor for a permanent memento of our highpoints venture, and before you could say Buffalo Bill Cody we were preparing our packs for the three-day hike to Kings Peak. At 13,528 feet, it's the highest point in the High Uintas Wilderness Area.

Kings Peak would be our twelfth highpoint. In the ten months since our last trip, we'd had to face some hard truths about how long this project would take, how much it would cost, and how much it would disrupt other aspects of our lives. Nels, a get-it-done-today kind of guy, was always pressing me to schedule our next trip. I'm the kind of person who can barely keep up with my laundry. My inability to make definitive plans was a source of constant irritation to him; his need to pin me down drove me nuts. The planning and phone calls were behind us, but while it felt good to be back on the road, the residue of conflict remained.

The slow-rising, narrow trail, which starts at roughly 9,500 feet, criss-crossed a creek for the first nine miles into a picturesque alpine bowl graced with small lakes and stands of pine, spruce, and fir trees. The hardest part of the first day's hike was fending off the man-eating mosquitoes that we slayed by the handful.

We set out early the following morning with stiff muscles and sore feet. The hike turned tough as we headed up and over Gunsight Pass, which tops out at 11,888 feet. The trail dips down before it climbs again and heads into a field in which the boulder-strewn path was marked by cairns. Negotiating this boulder field was an unexpected challenge. Breathless from the altitude, I stepped awkwardly from one rock to the next, feeling unsettled.

It took us five hours to cover the four remaining miles to the summit and three hours to get back down to camp. I threw my pack down and yanked off my dusty boots. The loose rocks on the backside of Anderson Pass made for a jarring descent, treating my feet like trespassers.

I pulled my sleeping bag outside the tent, reclined against a large rock and began shoveling handfuls of trail mix into my mouth. The sun on my face and bare, blistered feet felt luxurious. A nap was only minutes away.

"I propose we pack up and head back to the car," Nels said.

It was 3:30 p.m. The thought of breaking camp and hauling a fifty-pound pack nine more miles was repugnant.

"Let's go tomorrow," I said, hoping I sounded calm but firm.

Nels had an apparently overpowering need for a hot shower and soft bed. We debated the merits of staying versus leaving. But Nels was insistent.

I insisted on a short nap first. He took the word "short" literally and woke me fifteen minutes later. I packed up in a black mood.

By 4:30 we were back on the trail. Profoundly resentful, I surged ahead with the sole purpose of walking fast enough to punish Nels. Fatigue makes crank pots of the best of us. But the issues of comfort, cost, and control had been long simmering. On the road, Nels was inclined to eat less and spend money on motels. I preferred eating more and sleeping outside. Most of the time our differences complemented each other; on Kings Peak, given our fatigue, they brought our respective tempers to a near boil.

In his collection of essays, *Eiger Dreams,* Jon Krakauer writes, "By all accounts it is impossible for an extended two-person expedition to come off without inflicting permanent psychic scars on the participants if the weather turns grim." We'd been blessed with good weather, but Nels' Type A personality had precipitated a raging emotional storm in my Type B brain.

It took us four hours to make it back. Because I'd walked ahead, I waited for fifteen minutes by the car fending off a squadron of sinister mosquitoes. I really showed him, didn't I? When he finally arrived, we tossed our packs in the car and headed to town in silence. Halfway there, we heard the sickening sound of rim on road. I assumed that the flat tire was further punishment for our premature departure; although considering that I had to help Nels change the flat, the punishment lacked the specificity I desired.

After a shower and a very late dinner, we returned to our fleabag motel, where we lay on too-soft mattresses in the kaleidoscopic glow of the television and hashed out our differences. Nels complained that I was disorganized and unrealistic; I felt that he was too preoccupied with money. We talked for hours. To no one's surprise except our own, we were both right.

In the morning, all—well, almost all—of our grievances had been smoothed over. We had a huge breakfast at a truck stop and headed off to the Wind River Range and Gannett Peak. The sky was vast and the countryside glorious. In the bountiful scenery unfolding before us, our disagreements shrank to insignificance. Then I suggested stopping for a sandwich, and Nels said, "Whoa! That breakfast was supposed to hold you till dinner!"

He was joking, right? Yeah, he was. But for the moment I wanted to maim him. So when he ordered the six-inch sub and a large Coke, I made a point of ordering the twelve-incher and a cup of Utah tap water. ▲

WYOMING

Gannett Peak: *So Close Yet So Far*

The Western Swing

**Highest Elevation
13,804 feet**

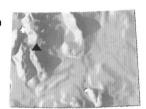

FROM THE TRAILHEAD to the summit of Wyoming's Gannett Peak and back is fifty miles—the longest roundtrip hike of any of the highpoints, including Denali. An hour up the trail we bumped into a couple headed out after thirty days in the Wind River Range. Their clothes tattered, they spoke like soldiers returning from the front—about "tons of snow" and whiteouts that left them tent-bound for days, lightning and thunder that rattled their fillings and frazzled their nerves, plus enough wind to last a lifetime. As we parted, the wiry woman with dreadlocks and a bandanna said, "I plan to become the drunkest hiker in town."

Unlike the neighboring Tetons, which leap from the plains in one dramatic thrust, the Wind River Mountains don't reveal their full splendor as you drive by on the deserted highways that parallel the range. Pretty, yes; magnificent, hard to say. But the farther you walk into the heart of this 110-mile-long range, the more remarkable it seems. No mountains in North America harbor more lakes. Despite the harsh weather, the alpine meadows are crowded with wildflowers. And the sharp, steep faces of the granite peaks that usher you into remote valleys are the stuff of rock climbers' dreams.

Of course, beauty can only take you so far. We needed to carry enough food and fuel to last three hungry hikers five days, and enough warm clothes to get to the top of a glaciated 13,804-foot mountain. Laboring in the July heat under sixty-pound-plus packs was hard work, made harder for Nels and me by the fact that our twenty-three-year-old guide, Ryan Hokanson, a climber, cyclist, and cross-country skier with bionic lungs, was cruising along the undulating trail like a trotter on a race track.

Toward the end of our second day on the trail, two scruffy ultra-marathon runners from Utah jogged up behind us. Like us, they planned to climb Gannett in the morning—only they would do it in the same skimpy running shoes they now wore (to which they would somehow attach crampons). One guy had climbed the mountain in 1984 and thought it was a harder climb than Mt. Rainier because of its knife-ridge. He confessed that Gannett scared him.

"So why climb it again?" I asked.

He gestured to the surrounding valley, the sun glimmering on the lake. Nodding toward his lean partner, he said, "I finally found someone dumb enough to go with me."

A few hours after they ran off, we set up camp at the far end of Titcomb Lake, a narrow, emerald-green body of water at 10,400 feet surrounded by steep, snowy 13,000-foot peaks. The valley was stark, windy, and inhospitable; the overall effect was stunning. The only sign of anything human was crude stone walls built to offer a tent shelter from the wind.

Much to my horror, Ryan's alarm sounded at 3 a.m. the next morning. It was Saturday, July 12, but as I willed myself out of my sleeping bag into the dark and cold, summer felt far away.

Wearing a headlamp and carrying a light pack, I headed into the blackness with a heavy dose of dread. Roughly forty-five minutes later we stood at the bottom of Dinwoody Pass. Solid steps had been kicked into the hard snow, so we left our crampons in our packs and slowly switch-backed up the steep, mile-long pass. At the top the wind was fierce. Below, it was light enough to see the Dinwoody Glacier, a barren but beautiful bowl marked by small crevasses.

We cruised down the back side, careful not to tumble. As the sun rose, we came upon a ditch, 100-feet deep and a quarter-mile long, shaped like a crescent moon, that the wind had tunneled out of the snow.

Around 9 a.m., after hiking to the base of a steep couloir (a narrow shoot of hard-packed snow and ice), we stopped, ate, and strapped on our crampons. The ever-mellow, laconic Ryan eyed dark clouds racing toward us and said, "Giddy-up." He was about as panicked as a man walking his dog.

Gannett was by far the most demanding of the peaks Nels and I had tackled together so far. Heading up the couloir I focused on Ryan's scuffed purple plastic boots, kicking into his steps and planting my ice axe into the hole left by his shaft. The incline was scary—so steep that any slip not followed by an immediate, well-executed self-arrest would result in a very long tumble that, if it didn't kill you, would likely leave you too broken to walk.

After two draining hours, we stood on an exposed ridge. In the couloir we had been sheltered; on top, the wind was nasty. And for the first time we saw the summit. While it was only 400 vertical feet away, to get there we had to follow a knife-ridge of snow, which fell off thousands of feet on each side. Looking at it made me queasy. While I remained silent, Nels said, "I have a bad feeling. I'm staying here!"

Ryan thought we had another hour to go. From where we stood, he said, it was impossible to assess the route up on the ridge. "If no one's been up there recently it could be tough in this wind."

I couldn't imagine not reaching the summit. We stood deliberating for about ten minutes. Ryan and I had decided to head up to take a look at conditions on the ridge when the wind intensified and snow began to fall. Nels said, "Let's go!" I nodded, and Ryan said, "We're outta here!"

To avoid the couloir, we headed down Gooseneck Glacier. It was now 11 a.m. and we were in the middle of a blizzard. Inching down the steep, knee-deep snow, I found it hard to stop thinking about those final 400 feet to the top. We had worked so hard and gotten so close. I had assumed—arrogantly, no doubt—that we would reach all the summits.

We headed back up Dinwoody Pass in the howling wind, weaving like drunks leaving a bar. At the top of the 13,000-foot pass, Ryan figured the wind at 70 mph. Snow raked the side of my face like sand. Visibility was less than ten feet.

We roped up and fought our way back down. Having just read Jon Krakauer's *Into Thin Air*, I flashed to the scene where retreating climbers caught in a storm were forced to spend the night exposed in conditions far harsher than those we now faced. And I also noted that if Nels and I had been on our own, we would have had a tough time finding our way back to camp.

By 3 p.m., eleven hours after setting out in the dark, we returned to our snow-encrusted tent. I was so wasted I struggled to untie the laces on my boots. We napped and ate and talked as the storm rattled on around us. Nels focused on how tense he'd been climbing unroped up the couloir; I obsessed about not reaching the summit. Ryan had stood on top several times so he didn't mind our hasty retreat. And Ryan had loved it all—the steepness of the couloir, the intensity of the storm. "It would be fun to do it in the winter," he said. Considering the old-fashioned ass-whuppin' we'd received, the idea nearly left me speechless. Was it a question of fitness, or experience, or did he just love mountains more than I did?

"Why would you want to climb this s.o.b. in the winter?" I asked.

"I dunno," he said. "I guess I enjoy the suffering."

He paused, probably aware of how weird that sounded. "I love the challenge of doing something hard."

For Nels and me, the challenge of climbing Gannett Peak in July had been more than enough. ▲

MONTANA

Granite Peak: *Fear with Gear*

**Highest Elevation
12,799 feet**

GRANITE PEAK is the only highpoint where climbers must tackle multiple pitches of vertical rock. It was first climbed in 1923, the last of the fifty state highpoints to be scaled. In *Climbers Guide to Montana,* Pat Caffrey says the stark 12,799-foot peak is known for its violent thunderstorms and offers climbers "a worthwhile confrontation"—rather daunting when you've climbed vertical rock a total of five times with all the confidence of a two-year-old on ice skates.

Five days after turning back from the summit on Gannett Peak in Wyoming, Nels and I found ourselves in the Beartooth Range at 10,500 feet on the barren, windswept, appropriately named Froze-to-Death plateau, again with Ryan as our guide. At 2:15 a.m., our second day on the mountain, the hiss of our propane stove and the whoosh of the wind filled our ears as we forced down oatmeal and dressed for the long day ahead.

For two hours we stumbled in the dark over and around boulders the size of refrigerators. Then Granite's massive northeast face appeared in the grainy gray light. The silhouette was jagged and the sheer, dark-brown rock face was streaked with ribbons of snow. Ryan eyed the wall and smiled. Nels stood silently taking pictures. I stared like a bystander at a traffic accident.

We headed down a 1,000-foot talus slope to a protected notch on the south side of the mountain where we changed into our plastic boots, climbing harnesses, and helmets. Gearing up, I kept asking our taciturn guide how hairy the route actually was. He assured us that the east side was "very doable." Yes, I thought, but for whom? In my mind, my shaky climbing skills and the fierce north face did not seem like a happy marriage.

Clearly, each of us brought different levels of experience and moxie to the mountain. Ryan, who had climbed the 13,770-foot Grand Teton more than forty times, was in his element. Nels, who had done a fair bit of rock climbing, was largely undaunted. I feigned composure but inside I was a basket case.

With this range of apprehension we set out across a curved snow bridge that led to the base of the rocky section of the climb. The bridge was roughly 100 yards long, as precipitous as the top of an A-frame roof, and dropped off to our left to a frozen valley 2,000 feet below. On the right it dropped at least 1,000 feet. Without a trace of irony, Ryan suggested that if we were going to fall, fall to the right.

Ryan led and placed protection. I followed. Nels took up the rear. Halfway across the snow bridge I slipped. I planted my ice axe and held on tight, but in a burst of adrenaline I emitted a yell that echoed across the valley, announcing to all that I was, in the words of Greg Child, "scared witless and shitless."

For five hours we moved higher and higher. To an experienced climber the route was easy. The hardest section was rated at 5.6. Not a problem if you're climbing in the Shawangunks in June. But we were climbing in plastic boots, in the cold, with gloves, above 12,000 feet, and with packs.

In virtually every photo that Nels took of me, my face is contorted in a grimace of abject terror. Even so, I could see that the scenery was stunning—sprawling glaciers and frozen lakes with patches of blue water in every direction. Along with the views, an image from that endless morning that sticks with me is Ryan smoothing his way up the craggy rock as if he were ascending an uneven flight of spiral stairs. At the end of each pitch I would struggle over a notch to find him sitting back, half bored, half bemused, pulling in the slack in the rope with a beatific, toothy grin.

Reaching the summit at 11 a.m., I felt relief rather than triumph. "We made it," said Nels.

Eyeing the dark clouds in the distance, Ryan said, "The hardest part is yet to come."

Nels took a few photos and Ryan, edgy for the first time, said, "Let's get the hell out of here before the lightning shows up."

Ascending had been tough but at least I could see the task at hand. Descending was like driving in Manhattan in reverse. When we crossed back over the snow bridge, I breathed a deep sigh and, for the first time, fully felt how hungry, thirsty, and tired I was. I walked the last five miles like a zombie. All I wanted was to curl up next to a rock and go to sleep.

We reached camp at 6:30, sixteen hours after setting out. There was

plenty of light, so we pulled our sleeping bags outside to lounge and eat and drink until we passed out like three men back from an all-night bender.

I woke at 9 p.m. under the misty glow of a near-full moon and walked to a nearby stream for some water. My legs were shot but I felt relaxed, even happy.

Just about everything about the day had been foreign to me: waking at 2 a.m., hiking over boulders in the dark, crossing the sharp ridge of a snow bridge to a wall of rock that vanished into the clouds. Risk-taking doesn't come naturally to me: Most of my urban relatives would consider this experience as foolhardy as fighting a bull without a sword. But while I'd been an emotional mess for much of the day, I felt that I had crossed a significant hurdle. The effort and focus required to get to the top had transformed fear into exhilaration. I didn't feel quite like my old self, and I liked it.

When I returned to camp, Nels was sitting up, with a bad case of hat head. He looked dazed. "How are you?" I asked, knowing that if his body felt anything like the way mine did when I woke up, it couldn't be that terrific.

"Just happy to be alive," he said smiling. He used a silly voice but he wasn't really joking. ▲

IDAHO Borah Peak: *Mortality on the Mountain*

**Highest Elevation
12,662 feet**

THE TWO-LANE HIGHWAY (U.S. 93) that runs through dusty Mackay, Idaho (population 537), might "go nowhere forever," as the leathery volunteer at the museum filled with mining memorabilia in town said. But for us it led to Borah Peak in the Lost River Range, one of the less-celebrated links in the chain of mountains that runs from the tip of South America through the Rockies to the top of Alaska.

Coming off arduous, multi-day climbs of Kings Peak (Utah), Gannett (Wyoming), and Granite (Montana), a one-day walk up the 12,662-foot Idaho highpoint seemed like a respite—with little apparent danger save for the thunderstorms that can scare the spuds out of a hiker high up on the barren mountain. In 1956, a climber was struck and killed by lightning on the summit.

However, after reading about the peak at the ranger station in Mackay, I began to feel less sanguine. In 1983 an earthquake registering 7.3 on the Richter scale struck below the mountain. As the rupture sped along the fault line it reached a speed of 5,000 mph, leaving a scar twenty-five miles long, ten miles deep, and dropping the valley more than seven feet. A hunter who watched the fracture rip across the hillside suffered whiplash as she clung to the sagebrush in the midst of the violent vibrations. She survived. The two school kids in town struck by collapsing masonry did not.

Clearly, the chance of another earthquake striking while we were there was as remote as an Elvis sighting but the obvious fact remained—a 12,000-foot mountain is not to be trifled with. Late in the afternoon the day before we planned to climb, we drove to Borah's trailhead to look around and met a grizzled man in his sixties coming down from the summit for the fifteenth time. Clad in blue jeans, a camouflage shirt, and a red bandanna under a baseball cap, he spoke of Borah as a friend, lover, and foe, regaling us with stories of the mountain's moods and geological nuances.

In 1984, he said, he was a member of a rescue team that went after two "kids" from Idaho Falls stuck out on Borah during a freak storm that raged for two days over Thanksgiving, plummeting temperatures to –40°F. "We didn't find the bodies until spring," he said, pointing over a rise where the two young men were found huddled together in the fetal position under a space blanket.

The next morning we set out with a healthier respect for what lay ahead, breathing hard as we walked up the steep, winding 3.5-mile trail. The climb was scenic yet uneventful until we reached the aptly named "Chicken Out Ridge." Many hikers who get this far peer over the intimidating drop to the right and decide to retreat. The name is tantamount to a dare, and some hikers who chose to brave the narrow, exposed trail have fallen and died there. I found ascending the 400 vertical feet daunting, but not hard. After seven hours of severe angst on Montana's Granite Peak, the so-called poultry section of the trail felt downright civilized.

At 11,989 feet we came to a snow bridge with steps kicked in near the sharply angled top. Shuffling across wasn't difficult, but the drop-off is so precipitous that a fall would spell disaster. On the other side was loose rock and scree, which covered the upper reaches of the southwest face of the mountain. Finally, five hours and 5,300 feet after setting out, we stood on top.

The view from the summit was a classic panorama of several 12,000-foot peaks. (Idaho's twenty-four highest mountains are in or border the Lost River Range District.) But that's not what I remember most about our stay on the top. While Nels roamed the summit's broad perimeter taking pictures, I sat and read the register, which was housed in a heavy black metal box.

Most of the entries were your typical, "Wow, I made it!" or "Glory to God" exclamations. However, one was a tribute to a twenty-three-year-old rock-climbing instructor named Jeremy Zaccardi. A year earlier, the Pocatello native died on Mt. Rainier from respiratory failure. "This was his home mountain," his girlfriend wrote. "He climbed it many times and had his first real mountain experiences here." In a few months, she wrote, a party would return to spread Zaccardi's ashes on the summit.

In a week, Nels and I would try to climb Rainier, so the death on that mountain's Emmons Glacier had personal relevance. But there was something else that intrigued me about this young mountaineer. Photocopied next to his obituary were some of his writings. His prose was a bit flowery—"I have signed a contract with them [mountains], and in them I will live out my life"—but he spoke about the basic reason climbers climb. "Powerful emotions are what a climber lives for," he wrote. "Fear and joy being the two strongest. Climbing is not a battle with the elements, or against gravity, it's a battle against oneself."

His words may not have been subtle or novel but, read on the peak of a mountain far from home, they felt very true. Failing to get to the summit in Wyoming, fighting fear on Granite in Montana, battling fatigue in Nevada and Colorado, these were battles Nels and I fought separately and together. But after each climb, the joy we felt was enough to explain why we—and Jeremy Zaccardi—kept coming back for more. ▲

OREGON Mt. Hood: *Doing it in the Dark*

The Western Swing

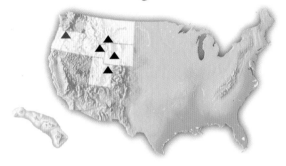

Highest Elevation 11,239 feet

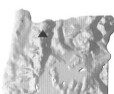

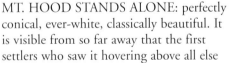

MT. HOOD STANDS ALONE: perfectly conical, ever-white, classically beautiful. It is visible from so far away that the first settlers who saw it hovering above all else as they pushed west on the Oregon Trail assumed it was just a few days' journey to the coast, when in fact they had weeks to go. Those who followed them across the plains in the nineteenth century longed to see this massive pyramid in the sky. To spot its distant white tip as they crested the Blue Mountains of eastern Oregon meant that their brutal trek—rife with food shortages, Indian attacks, and disease—was mostly over.

In 1833 the first serious bid to climb the 11,239-foot mountain was made by David Douglas, a Scottish botanist for whom the Douglas fir is named. But because his journal was lost when his boat (sans Douglas) was carried over a waterfall on the Fraser River in British Columbia, little is known of his failed attempt. Over the next twenty years, several parties tried and failed—or failed and claimed success. Finally, on July 11, 1857, four climbers clawed their way

to the top, suffering snow blindness in the process. Nevertheless, the Reverend T. A. Wood, a member of the team, wrote of the summit view, "Never in all my life have I seen a grander or more impressive sight."

Today, Mt. Hood is the most-climbed mountain in the United States—second in the world to Japan's Mt. Fuji. One reason is its accessibility from Portland and Seattle, hip cities home to almost as many outdoor enthusiasts as gourmet coffee shops. Even though Mt. Hood is a two-hour drive from Portland, the highly visible mountain seems part of the city. Whether you're stuck in traffic, rushing to a business appointment, or looking out your living room window, Mt. Hood's exquisite profile is right there, beckoning you closer.

During the three days Nels and I hung around town we must have said, "Wow!" or "Look at it now!" about every fifteen minutes.

We'd been on the road for twenty-three days before we arrived in Portland. We found a cheap motel on the outskirts of town adjacent to a topless bar, with—you guessed it—an impeccable view of Mt. Hood. While we'd been traveling hard and welcomed the rest, we would have hit the mountain sooner had we not been waiting for Nels' father, Dan, who was flying from Rockford, Illinois, to join us on Hood and Rainier, our last Northwest mountains.

An engineer by trade and flatlander by birth, the fifty-six-year-old father of three knew as much about climbing mountains as I did about building bridges: nada. He was an avid skier and had trained like a Trojan for this trip. But while he had the physical chops to get to the top, his healthy respect of high places bordered on mild panic. "I'm scared silly," he said whenever he saw Hood—again, about every fifteen minutes.

On Friday we spent the day practicing self-arrest and crampon and ice axe techniques on the soft, slushy snow with Steve Baldwin and Kirby Spangler of Timberline Mountain Guides. Roughly eight hours after the class, we were due back in the parking lot of the Timberline Lodge, an elegant stone building at the base of the mountain. By starting at midnight, we would be off the mountain before the sun melted the huge walls of rock and ice on the upper slopes and started the boulders bounding down the slopes like lethal bowling balls.

At 12:30 a.m. eight climbers and two guides crammed into the cab of a snow cat—a loud machine reeking of diesel fuel with the smooth ride of a military jeep on a rutted road. Unable to talk over the roar of the motor, we communicated with goofy grins and sign language as the cat groaned and slid to 8,500 feet.

We roped up in two teams of five and headed up the mountain at 1:30 a.m. The weather was perfect, 25°F and calm; the starry night sky was illuminated by a half-moon. This was the third time I'd started a climb in the

dark, but it still felt eerie trudging up a hard-packed glacier with no visibility beyond the arc of my headlamp. Save for the sound of my labored breathing and the gentle whir of the wind, we proceeded in silence.

The hike was hard but manageable until we hit a jagged snow ridge on the mountain called the Hogsback, which looked more like the dorsal armor on a stegosaurus than any porcine back I'd ever seen. We rested there in the dark, keenly aware of the hot sulfur stink belching from the steaming fumaroles—an obvious reminder that Mt. Hood is an active volcano.

We snaked up the southern face, negotiating our way around crevasses and chunks of ice as large as compact cars that littered the upper slopes. Dan swallowed his fear and did well, keeping pace with our swift-moving team. Finally, 5,300 feet from where we started, we stood on top and stared down on the twinkling lights of Portland fifty miles away. It was 4:15, forty-five minutes before sunrise.

I could hear voices and see the lights of other headlamps inching up to the summit. It was cold and still and exciting up there, looking out into a sea of nothingness. I felt a wave of expectation, like that portentous moment in a movie theater when the lights dim before the film begins.

Slowly, as the sun peeked over the horizon, the twisting Columbia River came into grainy focus. Then the truncated top of Mt. St. Helens, the youngest of the volcanoes in the Northwest, appeared, followed by Rainier and Adams—the so-called three guardians of the Columbia. As did Mt. Jefferson, farther off in the distance, and finally the rest of the lower Cascades.

Dan blurted out, "This is the thrill of a lifetime!" He was continuing a tradition of superlatives that had started in 1857 with the good Reverend T. A. Wood. ▲

WASHINGTON Mt. Rainier: *Getting High with Dad*

**Highest Elevation
14,410 feet**

ON JULY 4TH, a giddy group of would-be climbers from Illinois and I, the lone New Yorker, sat in Dan and Sara Akerlund's living room watching a Reader's Digest video on Mt. Rainier, the 14,410-foot extinct volcano that the Indians called Tacoma, "The Mountain," or "The Mountain that was God."

Months earlier, Dan Akerlund, Nels' semi-retired father, had decided he needed a new challenge and began training to join us on Hood and Rainier. Dan mentioned the trip to a co-worker who signed on and then recruited *his* best friend. Before you could say "on belay," seven of the nine slots in our five-day expedition seminar with Rainier Mountain Inc. (RMI) were filled with guys from Rockford—a small city where the biggest hill is the off-ramp on the interstate.

Watching the video with a roomful of nervous jokers was both amusing and humbling. As the baritone narrator spoke in grandiose terms about the power of a mudflow racing down the mountain like a raging river, uprooting trees and dislodging boulders, someone said, "I've got to remember to bring an extra pair of clean socks." An avalanche thundered down a slope and someone else cracked, "And extra tent poles!" The gallows humor reflected the obvious: We were novice mountaineers and this was a mountain for experts.

A month later, we met again in the parking lot outside Paradise Lodge, the grand hotel at the base of the mountain. As amazing as Rainier had seemed on video, it paled in comparison to the real thing, a mountain towering 9,000 feet above the surrounding foothills; an ever-white peak so big it's visible in any direction for 100 miles.

Except for Rainier and Denali, Nels and I had climbed every state highpoint out West. We'd traveled through America's biggest snow-capped mountains, but, with twenty-six glaciers on its flanks, nothing we'd seen loomed as large or was as awe-inspiring as the mountain overlooking Puget Sound. In *The Measure of a Mountain,* Bruce Barcott says of Rainier, "When it rises like a misshapen moon over downtown Seattle, the mountain entrances me, arrests my attention, and rouses my imagination; it makes me weave on wet highways."

The three RMI guides on our climb combed through our gear and divvied up our five-day supply of food and cooking utensils. I got to carry a pot large enough to bathe in. Trip leader Kurt Wedberg, a lanky Californian who had summitted Rainier eighty-six times, had climbed Mt. Everest in 1995. His two assistants, Matt Harmon and Chris Hooyman, had stood atop Rainier forty-seven times between them. (The record for Rainier summits at the time was 371, held by RMI guide Phil Ershler. His inscription in the summit log read, "371 and still fun!")

Except on Mt. Hood, where our group moved mostly in the dark and only for a day, Nels and I had climbed alone or with one other person. Being in a group of twelve guys for five days would be a new experience, and I wasn't sure I was going to like it. Luckily, the more we hung out, the more we worked together, the better we seemed to get along.

Some of this was due to the personalities on board—there were no egomaniacs, loudmouths, or crackpots to avoid—but the mountain gets most of the credit. To borrow the title of Peter Matthiessen's novel, we were at play in the fields of the lord. Day after day, sometimes hour by hour, the heavily crevassed, foreboding monolith delivered one awe-inspiring experience after another.

During the first two days of our climb the upper third of the mountain was covered by a mushroom-shaped cap known as a lenticular cloud, which is formed when the warm, moist air of the Pacific Ocean collides with the cold air over the mountain. On the morning of the third day—ta-da!—it vanished. It was the most dramatic unveiling you could hope for.

On our second night on the Kautz Route we camped at 9,600 feet on the Wilson Glacier in a snowfield known as the Turtle. After dinner, we sat around drinking hot chocolate and stared like stoned adolescents at an endless sea of clouds below us, bathed in orange and white and flamingo-pink light.

What made the beauty all the more compelling was the power within it— the sense that at any moment the mountain could squash you like a bug. Hanging on a rope fifty feet down a crevasse during a rescue drill, I glanced down and saw the walls of the blue ice disappear to blackness and felt my chest cavity constrict. The third time I was lowered into one of these gaping mail chutes to hell, I was nearly overwhelmed by the thought that the stunningly beautiful walls were closing in on me.

The following evening we were eating dinner at Camp Hazard at 11,600 feet when a serac, a wall of ice as big as a ten-story building, peeled off the cliffs directly above us and hurtled south with a sickening roar. Reasonably sure that we'd all be buried, I assumed a karate stance and froze like a startled deer. The ice crashed on a rock face and exploded. Tiny ice particles rained on us. "Cool!" said Kurt Wedberg, who'd seen similar wrecks countless times. He never flinched. "That was a big one."

On the mountain we developed a sense of what it means to be a team. At fifty-six, Dan Akerlund was our senior member. Dan had prepared diligently for the climb—circuit-training in a gym with a personal trainer and hiking daily in a park near his home with a pack filled with fifty pounds of rice. But he was mentally on edge and, with a painfully swollen right knee, a bit shaky on his pins.

Around dusk on our third day on Rainier, Kurt gathered us together to talk about our summit bid, which would start at 4 a.m. When he suggested we camp on the summit the following night—an ambitious project that would require good weather and a group strong enough to carry full packs to the top—Dan interrupted. "I can't make it. My knee is killing me!"

But Kurt believed he could, and so the rest of us convinced him to try. When we left our tents in the middle of a cold, starry night, a few of us shouldered some of Dan's gear to lighten his load. Climbing steep ice is a highly individual activity, but you could feel the group willing him up the slopes.

At 11:30 a.m., five-and-a-half hours after leaving Camp Hazard, we crested the south side of the crater rim and stood in the brilliant light on top of a shining world of ice and snow.

Everyone in the group exchanged high-fives and hugs. Nels and Dan embraced the longest. A video fantasy shared in the flatlands of Illinois had become reality on an icy crater in the Pacific Northwest. ▲

HAWAII   Mauna Kea: *Milky Way or Mars Bar*

The Western Swing

**Highest Elevation
13,796 feet**

YOU WANT BIG? From the base of the ocean floor to the highpoint marker on the red cinder cone known as Puu Wekiu, Mauna Kea is 33,000 feet, roughly 4,000 feet higher than Mt. Everest. Stand atop this gently rounded volcano and you are on the tallest mountain on Earth.

You want surreal? Mauna Kea is a tortured, red-brown-and-black boulder-strewn treeless landscape with a handful of bright-white domed observatories perched on top, housing the greatest collection of large astronomical telescopes on the planet. If you were standing twenty-seven miles away in lush Hilo, the "rainiest city in the U.S.," and were suddenly transported to the summit, you might believe you had landed on Mars.

I spent the month of March in Hawaii with my wife, Beth, and daughter Willa. Nels had shot Mauna Kea on a trip he'd taken months earlier. After three weeks of kayaking and (a little) writing on the island of Oahu, my family and I flew to the Big Island, also known as Hawaii. The only Hawaiian island with an active volcano, it is also the largest and most geographically diverse.

We drove north to the sleepy town of Honokaa, where we spent the night in a pleasantly ramshackle hotel that once housed cane and taro workers. The owner, a middle-aged Hawaiian woman from Maui, spoke to us about the native Hawaiian rights movement before sending us out to a local park with two wooden tennis racquets and a can of dead balls.

In the morning, we headed up Saddle Road, which cuts across the middle of the island. Because of frequent fog and rain, and the many sharp turns, accidents are common and the road is off-limits to rental cars without four-wheel drive (like ours). As we ascended, the lush greenery and ocean views yielded to a foreign, even hostile, lunar-looking landscape. Willa suddenly announced, "I don't like this place." By the time we reached the turnoff for Mauna Kea, she was complaining loud and often. Maybe it was carsickness, or the increasing altitude, or maybe she was more sensitive to the powerful vibes of the dormant volcano, but she made it clear that she wanted out—and fast!

The road to the summit looked even more forbidding, and the sight of it sent Willa into a near-panic—unusual for our normally easy-going kid. There was nowhere to leave them along Saddle Road. I drove on to Hilo, dropped my companions at a hotel, and headed back up Saddle Road into heavy rain and fog. Soon after mile marker 27, I made a right on the unmarked road toward Mauna Kea. Six miles later, at 9,240 feet, I turned into the parking lot of the Hale Pokaku Visitor Center. The air was cool; the sun nearly blinding.

In 1986, my brother and I had tried to drive to the top in a putt-and-sputter Rent-A-Wreck. The car never had a chance, and we turned back well short of the summit. This time I hoped to catch a ride at the Visitor Center with someone driving up in a four-wheel-drive vehicle. After chatting with a laconic fellow at the Visitor Center, I figured I'd drive as far as I could, stop when the car could go no farther and hike or hitch my way to the top. The Center sold Milky Way and Mars bars. I selected a Milky Way, grabbed some warm clothes from the trunk, and pulled my Nissan Altima onto the steep gravel road that vanished into the mist.

The tires spun and the car fishtailed, but moved forward.

Minutes later, I took my eyes off the road for a moment to look out over the precipitous drop-off to my right. Down below, the vast reddish-brown flank of the volcano disappeared into a thick sea of brilliant white clouds. I literally gasped. "Holy shit!" I murmured, the only phrase I could summon to capture the scene's grandeur. I found some classical music on the radio, cranked it as loud as it would go, and headed upward to what felt like a meeting with the great goddess of volcanoes, Pele, herself.

The terrain grew even more foreign. Enormous black boulders were strewn around like paper cups after a ball game; red cinder cones sprouted up all over like giant anthills. Finally, ten miles later, the gravel turned to pavement, the observatories sparkled in the bright, white light—and I was on top of the fiftieth state, 13,796 feet above sea level. Though Mauna Kea means "white mountain" in Hawaiian, there was no snow on the summit this day. When there is, locals like to drive to the top, fill a beer cooler with snow, and cruise back to sip cold ones on the beach.

The sky above Mauna Kea is above forty percent of the Earth's atmosphere and ninety percent of its water vapor. That means it's usually cloudless and very clear. I could see Maui in the distance and a crescent moon above. A ring of thick, puffy clouds hugged the middle of the volcano. The only sound was the faint hum of a generator and the crunching of volcanic stones under my feet.

Given how fast I'd gone from sea to summit, I felt light-headed, even tipsy. I wandered lazily around the prehistoric landscape until a lean man with a thick German accent and multi-colored jester's hat asked if I'd take his picture. He wrapped his arm around his blond companion and said, "Make sure you get Maui in the background."

He was a computer programmer; his tanned female friend was a jewelry maker from Maui who'd lived in about twenty-five different countries, including a lengthy stint in an ashram in India. We talked in reverential tones about Hawaii's magical allure, using the word "spiritual" so often we sounded like a brochure for a New Age retreat. We hugged when we parted.

An hour later I was back in Hilo.

Willa was happy to see me, and I her, despite how annoyed I'd been at the 54-mile detour she had required. Having been to the top, I could better understand why she'd felt so overwhelmed. Mauna Kea is a place of strange powers, and there was no point trying to convince her she'd just been carsick. So I told her how weird and wonderful it had been on top, and we talked about volcanoes. When I explained what a dormant volcano was, she perked up.

"Daddy," she said, "I think I was afraid it might wake up." ▲

INTO THE NORTHEAST

- New York
- Rhode Island
- Massachusetts
- Connecticut
- Vermont
- New Hampshire
- New Jersey
- Maine

NEW YORK
Mt. Marcy: *Sentimental Favorite*

Into the Northeast

**Highest Elevation
5,344 feet**

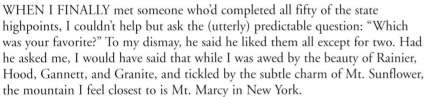

WHEN I FINALLY met someone who'd completed all fifty of the state highpoints, I couldn't help but ask the (utterly) predictable question: "Which was your favorite?" To my dismay, he said he liked them all except for two. Had he asked me, I would have said that while I was awed by the beauty of Rainier, Hood, Gannett, and Granite, and tickled by the subtle charm of Mt. Sunflower, the mountain I feel closest to is Mt. Marcy in New York.

At 5,344 feet, there are twenty-nine loftier highpoints. Though it's a long hike—anywhere from fourteen to twenty miles depending on the route—it's really not much more than a walk in the woods. And though it presides over a pristine wilderness, it's too well-traveled to feel very wild. But despite its modest stature, I'm still enamored with dear old Marcy.

Here's why.

In the mid-1980s my brother Marshall, a philosophy major at Northwestern University with a Zen Buddhist bent, had an existential crisis. One day during his senior year, he woke to the sickening realization that he had no interest in going to law school. Plan B was to become a stockbroker, make a

bushel of money in three years, quit, and use the savings to fund a long list of projects and adventures.

One of these was to purchase a dilapidated two-story house in the sleepy village of Saranac Lake, New York, 300 miles (and a world apart) from the apartment we shared in Brooklyn. He recruited me to assist with the renovation, and for nearly a year we worked like coolies and lived in rubble. But we fell hard for the Adirondack Mountains, a state park with six million acres—the largest protected wilderness area in the Lower 48. After work, we ran (or cross-country skied) on the trails, swam in the lakes (which doubled as a bath), and cycled the scenic backroads. We had found a land of recreational bliss—with no parking problems, street crime, or surly workers at the supermarket checkout. Motorists even stopped at intersections to let you cross the street.

One clear day in February, Marshall and I decided to climb Mt. Marcy. This was a bold mission for a couple of urban goofs. Neither of us had done much hiking in the winter. And although we loved to ski, when gravity was on our side we were dangerous on our $60 waxless skis. We owned snowshoes but had used them only a few times. While our hike up Marcy in February would not make climbing history, to us it was a daring ascent of personal significance.

It was a magical day—sunny and windless with heaps of snow and few people to disrupt our alpine adventure. When we stopped for lunch at Marcy Dam, roughly two miles up the trail, a small bird landed in Marsh's palm. Halfway up the mountain, when we could ski no farther, we donned our snowshoes and marched to the top through a wilderness wrapped in white.

The view was spectacular. Beneath our feet, an uninterrupted sea of snowy mountains, frozen lakes, and rivers spread out in all directions. It was so warm and windless on top that two guys sat shirtless sunning themselves. Our descent on skis, highlighted by several spectacular wipeouts, was a comic display that left us laughing like gibbering idiots.

Ten years later I returned with Nels and two friends to write a story for *The New York Times* on winter camping. We set up our tent in a lean-to in the High Peaks section of the park, roughly five miles from Mt. Marcy. Our itinerary was simple but fairly ambitious: on Saturday, hike Mt. Marcy; on Sunday, climb the northwest face of Mt. Colden, one of the premier mountaineering routes in the Adirondacks.

The narrow Indian Falls trail we followed to the summit of Marcy wound through stunted pines bowing under the thick layers of snow like a wedding cake frosted by a tipsy baker. The higher we walked, the smaller the trees became, until a trail-side sign announced we were in a fragile environment of arctic alpine pines.

We met three snow-encrusted parties who had retreated short of the summit. They told us visibility was nil; that winds of 50 to 70 mph had knocked them down. One of my friends had climbed all forty-six peaks in the park more than 4,000 feet. My other friend had spent a month alone in Montana's Glacier National Park, and his mountaineering skills more than made up for any Nels and I lacked. We chose to push on.

As soon as we left the shelter of the trees, our pristine winter wonderland turned hostile. We cleared snow off boulders to mark the way, took compass readings in case we got lost, and stumbled single-file in the knee-deep snow. Only when we bumped into a plaque that read "Tahawus"—Cloud Splitter, the Indian name for Mt. Marcy—did we realize that we were standing on top of New York. (Mt. Marcy was first climbed in 1837 by Ebenezer Emmons, a geologist who named the mountain after the New York governor who had appointed him a surveyor in the region.)

We huddled behind an outcropping of rocks. Unable to be heard over the howling wind, and with no view to admire, we were left with our own thoughts. "Man is nothing here, his very shouts die on his lips," the Rev. Joel T. Headley wrote after climbing Mt. Marcy in the 1840s. We lingered for twenty minutes in the storm. From tent to top and back took us seven hours.

That night I lay in my cozy sleeping bag in our frigid tent thinking about how many more wilderness experiences I'd had since Marsh and I had climbed Mt. Marcy that clear February day a decade earlier. I'd biked and kayaked across the United States and explored some pretty wild country at home and abroad. But it really all started in the Adirondacks, when my brother and I took a chance on climbing a 5,344-foot mountain in the dead of winter. Marcy rewarded our efforts beyond all expectation that day, and for that I'll always be grateful. ▲

RHODE ISLAND
Jerimoth Hill: *Fear and Loathing at 800 Feet*

Into the Northeast

**Highest Elevation
812 feet**

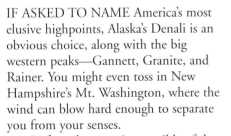

IF ASKED TO NAME America's most elusive highpoints, Alaska's Denali is an obvious choice, along with the big western peaks—Gannett, Granite, and Rainer. You might even toss in New Hampshire's Mt. Washington, where the wind can blow hard enough to separate you from your senses.

In fact, the most inaccessible of the nation's fifty highpoints is Rhode Island's 812-foot Jerimoth Hill. For years, it's been guarded by an antisocial homeowner who turns rabid when hikers cross his front yard en route to the highest point in the nation's smallest state.

From a journalist's point of view Henry Richardson's bad attitude is a blessing; if the seventy-seven-year-old retired music teacher weren't so cantankerous there'd be virtually nothing to write about. Strolling down the level, tree-lined path to the "top" (an elevation gain of fifteen feet) took us two minutes and thirty-six seconds—in flip-flops. Arriving at this flat, utterly unspectacular clearing in the woods, you're reminded of the line, "There's no there, there." The only feature of note is a battered green shed housing telescopes owned by Brown University. The two-foot-high slab of granite that is the official highpoint is so modest that most people feel compelled to quip that they made the ascent "without Sherpas or oxygen." The parking lot of my neighborhood supermarket has a better view.

Though eleven of the fifty highpoints in the country are on private property, the prickly situation in Rhode Island is unique. For years Dave Covill, co-editor of the 2,000-plus-member Highpointers Club magazine, tried unsuccessfully to negotiate dates on which Richardson would allow access to his property. Finally, in 1998, he struck a deal with Richardson's son, Ed, and hikers eager to get high in Rhode Island were granted permission to visit on a handful of national holidays. Prior to this agreement, the Highpointers Club considered standing next to the bullet-riddled highpoint sign on State Road 101 as the official summit.

After many months between climbing trips, Nels and I met in Providence on Labor Day and headed west on 101 for a possible encounter with the "madman of Jerimoth Hill." Though we'd approached several of our previous climbs with apprehension, this time man, not nature, was the source. I'd recently read a news item on the web ("Why Rhode Island's Molehill is the Nation's Toughest Summit") that reported, "Over the years Richardson has hurled insults, called the cops, threatened to break cameras, started fistfights." He's even quoted as saying, "Shoot all the damn highpointers!"

He wasn't kidding: We heard that several highpointers who'd tried to sneak by under the veil of darkness were shot at with rock salt. Richardson apparently monitors the path with motion sensors.

We arrived on a cool, rainy Monday morning and parked on a rise on the straight two-lane country road across the street from Richardson's red colonial house. Two sociable guys in raincoats stood in front of the wide trail headed into the woods.

One was an "official" highpointer acting as a liaison "to keep the peace." He expected anywhere from fifty to a hundred people, he said, although only fifteen had stopped by so far. The muscular redhead by his side was Gregory Griffith, a contractor from Jackson, Wyoming, who had just become the ninety-ninth person to complete all fifty highpoints. Griffith was a purist. Though he'd stood next to the sign marking the highpoint years ago, he had returned to stand on the "real" highpoint.

Were Richardson not a factor, most hikers would spend ten minutes making the round-trip walk (and many do). But the handful of open dates each year funnels so many highpointers onto Jerimoth Hill at the same time that lots of people just hang out to chat. We spent more than six hours there. While Nels searched for a defining shot, I talked to a steady stream of hikers who arrived like disillusioned trick-or-treaters. Virtually all of the people we met were highpointers; much of the conversation revolved around Richardson.

One fit-looking, chatty guy with close-cropped hair, who had forty highpoints under his belt, told me that when he was here in 1989 "someone" had let the air out of his car tires. Another reported that Richardson had chased a couple off his property and then pursued them in his car through three states. We heard about a cartographer who plotted a circuitous course through the woods to avoid Richardson's property. (Brown University actually owns the top; Richardson controls access to the trail that leads directly there.) Cunning cartographer that he was, he became so mired in a bog that he thought he was going to die there. It took him two hours to reach the top—scratched, muddy, and exhausted. Better he should have been shot at with rock salt.

There were five open dates this year. Each was well attended, and each, according to a highpointer volunteer I spoke to, has gone off without a hitch—except for the day the Old Man came charging out of the house early in the morning screaming, "Get the hell off my property!" Once he was reminded that

it was an agreed-upon open date, he retreated.

The irony, of course, is that Richardson's antics on Jerimoth Hill have brought more attention—and people—to the place he so desperately desires to protect. We stayed long after Nels had taken his last photo, hours after we'd said we really should get going, because the conversations that continued around the small rock at the top were hard to walk away from: the loud Texan joking about his struggles on Mt. Kilimanjaro, the beaming eight-year-old boy from Illinois who'd notched his first highpoint, Greg Griffith advising us about Denali. This rainy day in Rhode Island had been transformed into an impromptu highpointers' convention.

People compared notes, exchanged e-mail addresses, and made plans to climb together. While Nels and I had already climbed nearly two dozen highpoints, this was the first time I felt excited about being part of an eclectic community—sort of like when you meet a person from your home state in a foreign country. Our common bond was the desire to stand atop all fifty of America's highpoints. Whether we would all make it or not was less important than the desire to try. And maybe what tickled me most was that all of this highpointing enthusiasm had converged on an 812-foot hill, a sharp stone's throw from a man who'd never met a hiker he wouldn't like to pelt. ▲

MASSACHUSETTS
Mt. Greylock: *The Mountain of Metaphors*

Into the Northeast

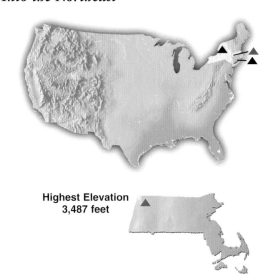

Highest Elevation
3,487 feet

MT. GREYLOCK is a beacon. The stone monument on the summit looks like a giant rook on a chessboard. This imposing war memorial, which sits just off the Appalachian Trail, is a popular hiking destination "only" 589.9 miles from the end of the line at Mt. Katadhin in Maine. Motorists seeking a majestic view arrive via the winding road. Cyclists seeking strain ride to the summit. However, if you're seeking solitude, look elsewhere. The parking lot on Mt. Greylock is rarely empty.

We left Jerimoth Hill late in the afternoon and drove west to Mt. Greylock, located in the northwest corner of Massachusetts. Though I grew up in the East, I'd never heard of Mt. Greylock. At 3,487 feet, I expected a thoroughly unremarkable mountain.

I was wrong. At a clearing near the top, the view stopped us in our tracks. It was, as Henry David Thoreau described, an "ocean of mountains" that disappeared before us in wave after shaded green wave.

"Wow," I said.

"Big wow!" Nels replied.

We arrived on top at around 5 p.m. Rounding the last turn, the monument nearly assaults you. The drab stone structure is so large and official-looking you'd think you were in Washington, D.C., rather than the only sub-alpine environment in Massachusetts. Though it seems out of place, there's been a tower of some kind on the summit since 1833. In 1878, a 60-foot wooden tower built as a weather observatory burned down. It was replaced by an iron tower in 1889. In 1931, a lighthouse originally slated for Boston Harbor somehow was adapted as a war memorial and placed atop Greylock.

That quirky shift of venues makes a little more sense given Greylock's many literary connections to the sea. Herman Melville, the author of *Moby Dick*, set up an observation deck at his home in Pittsfield in order to gaze at the mountain. While it sounds like a load of sperm oil, it's said that Greylock's humpback profile was part of the inspiration for Melville's great white whale. (Greylock is a monadnock, a fancy way to say that it's visible from all four directions.)

Nathaniel Hawthorne, who gave us plenty of Puritan angst in *The Scarlet Letter*, described the summit view as "huge mountain swells heaving up…[with]

waves far and wide around it." And Thoreau, who huddled under boards to stay warm during his night on the summit, wrote about the "ocean of mist, which by chance reached up to exactly the base of the tower, and shut out every vestige of the earth…."

I trudged up the tight spiral staircase to the top of the 92-foot lighthouse. To the north, Vermont's Green Mountains faded into the horizon; the Berkshires and Catskills disappeared to the south. Everywhere you looked were mountains and valleys and water. The unexpected force of the view explained why folks have been making poetic proclamations about this 3,487-foot mountain for generations. In 1906 John Bascom, the first superintendent of the state park system, said Greylock is "…our daily pleasure, our constant symbol, our ever renewed inspiration for all who have fellowship with Nature."

After twenty minutes in the tower, a thick mist blew up from the valley and wrapped the mountain in white. While some say that the mountain was named after Chief Greylock, the leader of the Mohawk Indians who once inhabited this area, others say it's because the mountain is continually locked in gray clouds. (When we returned the following day, dense clouds dominated the mountain, giving some credence to the latter theory.)

Back on terra firma, I found the Appalachian Trail and wandered down its winding path a short distance, wondering how different this experience would be had I walked here from Springer, Georgia, 1,554.1 miles away (the sign in Bascom Lodge, just below the monument, gives the exact mileage).

Dusk was firmly upon us and though it had been a warm September day, the wind picked up and the temperature fell fast. The monument's beacon cast a diffuse, eerie glow on the mist settling thickly around us. The light, visible seventy miles away, was once the most powerful in Massachusetts. As Nels took pictures, I sat on the low stone wall surrounding the monument. Nearby, a mother in a Navy sweatshirt chased her rambunctious three-year-old boy. She let it be known that she was concerned about her husband, who was cycling up the road in the fog and encroaching darkness. "I can always call him on the cell phone," she anxiously told her carefree child.

By 8:00 Nels had joined me under the monument. Compared to the sociable, decidedly non-poetic scene atop Jerimoth Hill where we had spent much of the day, the peaceful tower with its incandescent halo seemed that much more surreal.

"Get what you need?" he asked.

I nodded.

We stared at the stars that appeared in a clearing. A sweaty man in biking garb emerged from the darkness and stepped into the light like an actor coming on stage. "Excuse me," he said, blinking. "Have you seen a woman and a little boy?" I suggested he check the lodge. "If she's not there," I said, "call her cell phone."

He trudged off on heavy legs to find his family; we drove down the mountain in search of a large seafood pizza. ▲

CONNECTICUT

Mt. Frissell: *Therapy with a View*

Into the Northeast

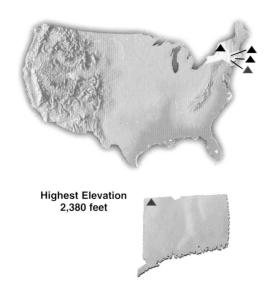

**Highest Elevation
2,380 feet**

MT. FRISSELL IS A MODEST MOUNTAIN with pretty, OK, extremely pretty, views in a pretty part of the state. That's not a ringing endorsement, I know, but at just 2,380 feet—the thirty-fifth-tallest state highpoint in America—Mt. Frissell is not a mountain that inspires hyperbole. And the name—rhymes with fizzle—probably doesn't help. Tucked away in the northwest corner of the state, Frissell supposedly receives fewer visitors than just about any other highpoint in the country.

Mt. Frissell suffers another minor indignity. Five miles away on the Appalachian Trail, a sign states that Bear Mountain is the highest peak in Connecticut. In fact, Bear Mountain, which is sixty-four feet lower, is the highest mountain *completely* within the state. Nevada and Connecticut are the only two states with highpoints on mountains whose actual summits are over the state line. So while the highest point in Connecticut is the south slope of Mt. Frissell, the mountain's true summit is a few feet north in neighboring Massachusetts.

On the flip side, the drive from Mt. Greylock south through the Berkshires on Route 7 was postcard pretty. And the country around Mt. Frissell was far more wooded and remote than I had imagined. In Salisbury, a quaint old town (the birthplace of Ethan Allen, the leader of the Green Mountain Boys), we turned off onto a rocky, one-lane dirt road and drove uphill alongside a rushing stream. The woods thickened as we climbed. I kept repeating, "I can't believe this is Connecticut."

At a pristine lake, we turned right onto Mt. Washington Road. Two rutted miles later we parked at a small clearing. We stopped at the weathered granite obelisk marking the juncture of New York, Massachusetts, and Connecticut; found the trail marked with red splotches; and continued on with overly modest expectations. I wore sandals.

The trail passes through three states. It's roughly a mile and a half to the summit with an elevation gain of less than 600 feet. The hike is as pleasing as it is unremarkable. ("Nice brook." "Hey, look at the fungi on that tree.") I'd read that black bear, bobcat, wild turkey, deer, raccoon, and grouse roamed these parts but we saw nothing larger than a chubby chipmunk. We scrambled up a short, steep section of sparkling quartz near the top, bashed through some prickly holly bushes and arrived at the small rock cairn on Frissell's south slope.

"Well?" I said.

"It's nice," Nels said.

The view was awfully nice—the Catskills to the west, the Hudson Highlands to the south and the Berkshires to the north. Nels sighed. There was no defining shot, nothing that said, "I am Frissell, hear me roar!"

The wind was gusting to 25 mph. It was cold. The trees on top were stunted. Diminutive Mt. Frissell had an alpine feel on top. We had the summit to ourselves. Nels took pictures; I squatted behind a boulder for a windbreak and stared out at the bald peaks, watching birds glide over valleys graced with trees and water. Some of the foliage had already changed color. It was early September, and fall felt near.

An hour later, Nels shouted my name. He was on his belly photographing the skin of a rattlesnake. It was translucent and separating like layers of a delicate pastry. "At home I'm always racing like a madman," he said. "This is so therapeutic for me."

Nels continued hunting for photos and I returned to my rock—just listening and looking and thinking. Mountaintops provoke introspection. Perhaps it's the silence; perhaps it has to do with staring off into the distance high above the material world. It's as the critic and philosopher John Ruskin said, "Mountains seem to have been built for the human race as at once their school and their cathedral."

My thoughts turned to my mother, who had died six months earlier from pancreatic cancer. Before her diagnosis, she was one of the healthiest, hardest-working, and most energetic people I knew. We learned of her illness in February; in March she died from an embolism lodged in her lung. She was sixty-four.

On the big peaks out West I'd been impressed by the number of inscriptions in the summit register paying homage to the dead. Often these notes gave credit to a loved one for providing the inspiration to get to the top. Shortly after my mom's death I climbed two big volcanoes in Ecuador. I'd spent a lot of time thinking about her on that trip, but above 18,000 feet when the going got tough I had to focus on avoiding crevasses and trying to put one foot in front of the other. Here on Mt. Frissell, where the air was rich and the view both subtle and sublime, I felt her presence, or at least an overwhelming wave of sadness that had become familiar over the past months.

Observing the intricate relationship between life and death in nature has always comforted me. Most of us are afraid of change, of death. "We fear death because it is unknown," writes Paul Rezendes in *The Wild Within*, "and the unknown is where thought cannot go." In the woods there is a simplicity and lack of sentimentality about the way one creature's death provides sustenance for another. This awareness wasn't easing my sorrow now, but it was, well, therapeutic to sit here with my sadness in this peaceful, private place. I cried and smiled and asked aloud, "What happened, Mom? Where did you go?" I'd spent a lot of time wondering why she'd died so young, but I wasn't really looking for answers on this bald, windy summit tucked in the corner of Connecticut, only a place to visit with my mom.

When Nels shouted that he was ready to go, we'd been on top for more than two hours. We didn't talk much on the way down, but it was obvious that our respective attitudes about the mountain had changed. Halfway down, Nels set up his tripod next to a rushing brook. He shoved a pinch of chewing tobacco under his lip, turned his cap backward and said, "I just love this shit!"

Knowing we'd be here a while, I sat and began studying the lichen in a crack in the rock. "Therapeutic," I said. "Very therapeutic." ▲

VERMONT

Mt. Mansfield: *Misty Memories*

Into the Northeast

**Highest Elevation
4,393 feet**

WHEN I WAS A KID, my Uncle George, a combative lawyer who slept four hours a night and drank coffee hot enough to melt steel, lived in a 200-year-old farmhouse on 100 acres outside of Rutland with his wife Lillian. A native New Yorker, he loved to say that Vermont had more cows than people. While that might have been true during the 1970s when we often visited, a 1995 census for the Green Mountain State reported that Homo sapiens outnumbered their bovine brethren, 584,771 to 310,518.

Heading up Route 91 to fetch Nels at the Burlington Airport on a beautiful afternoon in October, I thought about my (now long gone) uncle. Visiting that classic farmhouse was like stepping back in time: There was a pot-bellied stove and rough-hewn beams in the kitchen and no TV. When you picked up the phone someone was usually chatting away on the party line.

My uncle loved the seclusion and stillness and sanity of life in the sticks. A Socialist in the twenties, he appreciated Vermont's progressive politics, Yankee libertarianism, and the fact that the locals tolerated the hippies who flocked to Vermont in the sixties. He was proud that the citizens of Vermont refused to permit billboards on the highway. Even today, Montpelier is the country's only state capital without a McDonald's.

I liked it because on hot summer days my brother and I hiked up a frigid, boulder-strewn stream that flowed down the mountain. Some days we ventured deep into the woods until we were nearly lost. I milked my first cow there and drove my uncle's Jeep on a frost-buckled dirt road when I was twelve. And, at age fifteen, I participated in my one deer hunt—a silent, manly procession framed with excitement and fear that remains one of my most memorable walks in the woods. (For the record, I didn't hit a tree, much less a deer.)

Nels and I spent the night in Stowe, a trendy ski resort town eight miles from Mt. Mansfield, and headed up the Long Trail on a wet, raw Thursday morning. The 270-mile trail, which overlaps the Appalachian Trail for 100 miles in southern Vermont, traverses the main ridge of the Green Mountains from Massachusetts to Canada.

At 4,393 feet, the twenty-sixth-tallest state highpoint, we didn't expect Mansfield to be terribly strenuous. But in the rain, the slick path, which gains 2,800 feet in just 2.3 miles, turned steep fast. Less than a mile up the trail, we scrambled onto a large slab and broke through the trees to a rocky landscape wrapped in mist and fog.

Viewed from the east, Mansfield's two-mile-long profile purportedly looks like a face (especially if you've been drinking heavily). At the southern end of the ridge is the broad, flat Forehead, then the Nose (the cluster of transmission towers on the proboscis are the Nose Hairs), and Mansfield's Kirk Douglas-esque summit, the Chin. The bump below is the Adam's Apple. However, on this gray October day, all we saw were stunted trees and a steep slope littered with slick boulders speckled green.

The wind became more of a force as we climbed. The wild mood swings of weather were part of what I remembered most from my childhood visits to Vermont—like the time Friday's snow flurry turned into Saturday's state of emergency. Blissfully stranded 250 miles from our school, my brother and I spent three days speeding down the middle of the road on a toboggan.

The fog on Mansfield was so thick Nels and I didn't realize we were on top until we could go no higher. According to one guidebook, the arctic-alpine tundra up there is normally found 1,500 miles to the north in Canada. The average wind speed on top is 26.5 mph; on this day it was so strong I could spread my arms, lean into the wind like a ski jumper and remain upright. A few minutes after we arrived, the rain turned to hail.

Suddenly the fog lifted and the sun poked through, and a glorious tapestry of fall colors appeared. Then, before you could say Ethan Allen and the Green Mountain Boys, another curtain of clouds descended and we were socked in again until we were assaulted by the next burst of sun. In an essay entitled "Natural Light: Life among Vermont's hippies, hunters, bears and moose," Edward Hoagland called "the rolling weather so dependably unpredictable that it jounces you as air pockets do a plane."

I still visit Vermont regularly. My brother, another solitary-minded soul—part social reformer, part crank, part Buddhist—carries on the tradition, living with his wife and two daughters in a log house on five acres in the woods twenty miles from Brattleboro. And if he can't brag, as Uncle George did, that cows outnumber people in Vermont, he can still point out that the highest ratio of cows to people belongs to one of the sanest, most scenic states in the country. ▲

NEW HAMPSHIRE Mt. Washington: *The Windiest Place on Earth*

Into the Northeast

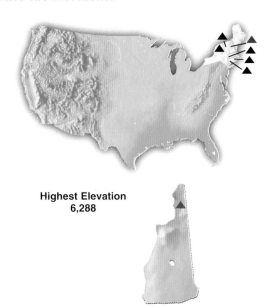

**Highest Elevation
6,288**

THE TOUR BUS CHUGGED up the winding road to the top of Mt. Washington. I sat sweating in the back, trying not to vomit. Like all self-respecting highpointers, Nels and I had planned to hike to the summit. However, the day before (in an all-day rain), we'd climbed Mt. Mansfield, the highpoint in Vermont. By the time we arrived in North Conway it was 2 a.m. When the alarm sounded at seven the next morning we conveniently forgot to wake up. Before you could say Jefferson, Madison, and Adams, the morning had slipped by.

Without adequate daylight to hike round-trip, we opted to take the shuttle bus to the top and hike down. Nels, who had climbed the mountain in college, had no problem with the ethics of this as long as he returned with solid photographs. But I had never climbed the mountain before, although years ago I'd attempted it on an eighty-degree day only to be turned back halfway up by golf-ball-sized hail. While our schedule more or less dictated that we hitch a ride to the top, I felt like I was cheating on a final exam. I could have been enjoying the crisp, clear October day on the trail. Instead, I endured a serious dose of carsickness as our jovial tour guide regaled us with the following facts:

• Construction on the road up Mt. Washington began in the 1840s. It is the oldest man-made tourist attraction in the country. The road was opened to the public in 1861. Back then, the twelve-mile ascent in a horse-drawn covered wagon took four hours and cost 32¢. (On foot it was 16¢.) Today it's $22.

• The record for the fastest ascent on a bicycle is 50 minutes, 20 seconds, set by professional cyclist Tyler Hamilton. The fastest runner logged 58 minutes, 21 seconds. Our bus climbed to the top in 12 minutes, 40 seconds.

• The warmest temperature ever recorded on top was 72°F; the coldest air temperature –47°F. The highest wind speed, 231 mph.

The hike down was pretty but the overall experience was uneventful and left me wanting more.

I got more—and then some.

Four months later, on a clear day in January, my wife Beth and I returned with guide Maury McKinney, who runs the International Mountain Climbing School in North Conway. As we drove to the snowy mountain on a cold Tuesday morning, Maury offered a few more facts about the 6,288-foot mountain. While Mt. Washington receives an average of 256 inches of snow each year, he said, it's best known for the wind, gale force on an average day and hurricane force about every third day. The statistics show that Mt. Washington is potentially dangerous at any time of the year. The combination of easy access and dangerous weather gives it one of the highest casualty rates in the world. And the weather was generally the most dangerous in January.

At 9:30 a.m. we started from Pinkham Notch, elevation 2,032 feet, on the wide Tuckerman Ravine Trail. If all went well, we'd be back in eight or nine hours. Two miles and forty-five minutes later, we had gained roughly 1,500 feet. We turned off onto the Lion Head winter trail, a narrow, steep track through thick woods, where the danger of avalanches was low.

Just below tree line we met a lone climber, who moved aside to let us by. With ice hanging from his beard and hair, he looked as if he'd just emerged from a snow cave. He muttered something about 90 mph winds and blizzard conditions. Maury smiled like a crossing guard and kept moving.

Soon the trees shrank to just a few feet high. On a wide, open slope littered with snow-covered rocks and boulders, the fabled wind raced down to meet us like a rabid dog. After three hours of slogging into this 40-60 mph tempest, the left side of my face turned gray and numb. (We learned later that the temperature with windchill was –57°F.)

At times the snow was thigh deep; sometimes our crampons clattered on bare rock. In the fog and blowing snow, visibility was only about fifty feet. For Beth, who weighs less than 130 pounds, the going was tough. With about a mile to go, I asked her if she wanted to continue. Later she said, "I didn't want to *go* down; I wanted to *be* down." She gamely trudged on.

We were the only climbers to reach the top that day. The summit, which had bustled with buses and cars and camera-wielding tourists in the fall, was now abandoned, with hoarfrost clinging to every structure. The cold penetrated my Gore-Tex shell; the wind felt nearly suffocating. We huddled behind a closed concession stand and sipped hot tea, but it felt dangerous not to move.

The trip down was a gift. Maury bounded through the deep, powdery snow like a schoolboy. Where the slope was steep enough, we sat down and slid. My fingers and toes warmed up. The wind and gravity were on our side. Back in the parking lot, we hustled into the car and cranked up the heat. This time when we drove off I felt profoundly fulfilled. I was twice as tired but had experienced not even the mildest dose of carsickness. ▲

NEW JERSEY

High Point: *Reconstruction Is No Laughing Matter*

Into the Northeast

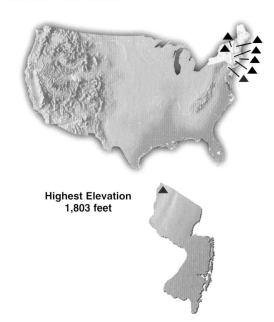

**Highest Elevation
1,803 feet**

NEW JERSEY IS ONE of the thirteen original states. Grover Cleveland, the twenty-second and twenty-fourth President of the United States, was born in Caldwell, New Jersey. The first submarine, *Miss America*, and the first drive-in movie theatre are credited to the Garden State. The nickname actually fits—the state has 9,500 farms and ranks second in the country in the production of blueberries. Still, most of the country sees the state as the "armpit of America" and jokes accordingly. As a native New Yorker, I've been hearing—and making—Jersey jokes all my life.

Much of the abuse is directed toward the rancid-smelling industrial corridor south of New York City along the New Jersey Turnpike. While some of it is New Yorkers (like me) making a scapegoat of their diminutive neighbor, there *is* something quintessentially Jersey-esque about New Jersey that lends itself to mockery.

The state highpoint, located fifty-eight miles from Newark in the northwest corner of the state, is in High Point State Park. The fact that this 1,803-foot hill (the eleventh lowest) is named "High Point" reveals a certain, shall we say, literal quality that characterizes the state. An Internet search revealed over forty area businesses with "High Point" in their name. My favorite is the High Point Wheat Beer Co., although High Point High School runs a close second.

Nels and I arrived on a snowy Saturday in early March. The parking lot at the High Point Cross Country Ski Center was nearly full. The two-lane road that wends its way to the top deposited us in an empty lot with huge banks of snow pushed off to the side. A short walk away stood a 220-foot obelisk surrounded by scaffolding and ringed by a chainlink fence. At the ski center, it was clear and sunny; near the monument, a three-minute drive up the road, the wind made it twenty degrees colder.

A few moments after we arrived on top, a procession of gleaming VW Passats streamed in and parked with military precision in two diagonal lines of eight. The drivers, members of a local car club out for a jaunt, hopped out, took some photographs (of their vehicles, not the view), and sped off.

"Weird," Nels said.

"New Jersey," I replied.

It took us a few minutes to walk uphill to the fenced-off area. The wind racing through the scaffolding surrounding the tower made a high-pitched screeching sound like a tea kettle at full boil. According to the *Newark Star-Ledger*, this mini–Washington Monument was erected in 1930 in memory of New Jersey's wartime heroes. The restoration of the crumbling granite exterior and rusting metal staircase began in 1998 and will cost an estimated three million dollars—a tab that includes replacing the 600-pound bronze door that was stolen in 1997.

"They stole the door?" Nels asked.

"Jersey," I replied.

Had we been able to climb all 291 steps, we would have had a stellar view of the Poconos to the west, the Catskills to the northeast, and the Wallkill River valley to the southeast. Instead we lingered around the fence and listened to the fierce wind. We wandered around the parking lot and stared out over the panorama of snow-capped rolling hills, our eyes tearing from the wind.

We drove back down the hill. When Nels walked across frozen Lake Marcia to photograph the monument, I headed to the Cross Country Ski Center. Inside, rosy-cheeked skiers chowed down in a cozy room with large windows that perfectly framed the obelisk. A video of the fifty-kilometer cross-country ski race from the Olympics in Lillehammer played on a TV high on the wall. On the screen thousands of flag-waving, bell-ringing, screaming Norwegians—some shirtless (read, drunk), many with their faces painted to look like their nation's flag—stood three deep exhorting their well-tuned cardiovascular heroes ("Bjorn!" "Jan!") to prevail.

I experienced a moment of geo-cultural disorientation. This was Jersey; there should have been a Jets game on the TV with the crowd yelling, "Yo Vinny, you suck!" Or, "We luv ya!" depending on the outcome of the play. Maybe it was the effect of the microclimate. High Point, New Jersey, claims the distinction of being "the snowiest spot in the metropolitan area," which was no doubt the reason that Hans Petter Karlsen, former world-class Nordic skier and director of the ski center, made it his home. Now High Point also can boast that it has "the longest cross-country ski trail in the United States covered by snow-making."

I mentioned this fact to Nels as we drove down into the macroclimate to find lunch.

"Bizarre" he said.

"New Jersey, my good man," I replied. "New Jersey." ▲

MAINE Mt. Katahdin: *The Beginning or The End?*

Into the Northeast

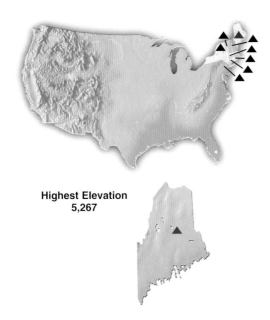

**Highest Elevation
5,267**

AT A SCENIC STOP along Millinocket Lake, two dozen miles south of Mt. Katahdin, we stopped to study the band of mountains that towers over Baxter State Park. A lanky, balding, bearded cyclist smoking a hand-rolled cigarette stared at the mountain. Given his tan and the size of the trailer he was pulling, it appeared he'd been on the road for weeks. In fact, he'd started in Virginia and had been riding along the Appalachian Trail for two months. Pointing to a jagged bump—Katahdin's Baxter Peak—he spoke like a bad actor reciting Shakespeare, using broad, sweeping hand gestures. "That's my destination!" he said, smoke pouring from his nostrils. "I've spent so much time thinking about this place. I find it difficult to believe that I'm almost there." He punctuated his statement with an expletive, or three.

Halfway through our conversation, we were joined by a man who'd grown up in Millinocket, a mill town twenty-two miles from Baxter State Park. "I know this mountain," he said several times with a pronounced Maine accent. He spoke of Katahdin's multiple moods—snow storms in July, deadly lightning strikes on the Knife's Edge, and winds fierce enough to pin a moose

in a phone booth. "Even people who live around here don't know how incredible she is," he said. "I know this mountain. I grew up right here in Millinocket."

"It's beautiful!" said the cyclist, with yet another expletive.

"Ayuh, it is," said the Mainer with profound satisfaction.

I grew up in New York. Until we started climbing highpoints, I knew little about Katahdin (the Abenaki Indian word for "greatest mountain"), save that it was the northern terminus of the Appalachian Trail, 2,150 miles from Springer, Georgia. After Mt. Washington in New Hampshire, Katahdin is the most renowned and formidable mountain in the East. Its boulder-strewn slopes and a precipitous mile-long ridge, known as the Knife's Edge, are its defining features. Though I knew all of this when I picked up Nels at the airport in Portland, I was stunned by the breadth of its steep, broken gray headwalls, which dominated the otherwise flat northwoods. With roughly 3,800 feet of exposed rock above tree line, the sheer, jagged 5,267-foot highpoint reminded me of a scaled-down version of the Tetons.

The day before our climb, we drove into the park to look around. A ranger told us there was a seventy-percent chance of thundershowers—bad news if we planned to hike the Knife's Edge. We did. She told us about the heavy wind and terrifying exposure, and a Boy Scout killed by lightning. She painted so vivid a picture of hiking the ridge in foul weather that I rolled up my window as we drove off, even thought it was 70°F, a postcard-perfect day in early September.

Fortified with Gore-Tex rain gear and a healthy dose of paranoia, we arrived at the park entrance at 6:30 a.m. the following morning. At the trailhead at the Roaring Brook Campground, the parking lot bustled with hikers sipping coffee and readying their gear. Considering that we'd hardly seen a dozen cars in one place since we'd been in Maine, the mob scene was nearly unsettling.

It was cool and overcast as we headed down the Chimney Pond Trail. After 3.3 mostly easy miles up a rocky, well-worn trail that followed a stream, we came to a clearing known as the Great Basin where we would pick up Cathedral Trail, our route to the summit. We ate lunch and basked in the magnificent view of the broad massif. The steep-walled cirques and serrated ridges were almost surrounded on three sides by a ring of lower summits. It was unlike any piece of geology I'd seen in the East. While Katahdin was spectacular from afar, from this vantage point it was even more inspiring. As hikers arrived at the clearing, they invariably stopped to gawk. We spoke to a father and his teenage daughter who have climbed the peak each Labor Day for the past five years, and to a group of six friends who have also made it an annual pilgrimage. They confirmed what seemed obvious from where we sat—we had a whole lot of mountain left to climb.

Paul Zumwalt, author of the guidebook *Fifty State Summits*, called the hike "the most difficult of the state summits east of the Mississippi." Though the book was a valuable resource, I tended to think that Zumwalt generally overestimated a climb's difficulty. Halfway up the Cathedral Trail, I realized I owed Mr. Zumwalt an apology. Henry David Thoreau, who climbed Katahdin in 1846, described the precarious routes up the mountain best, "The mountain seemed a vast aggregation of loose rocks, and they lay as they fell on the mountain side, nowhere finally at rest, but leaning on each other all rocking stones, with cavities between, but scarcely any soil or smooth shelf…this was an undone extremity of the globe." Said simply, the "trail" (marked by blazes painted on rock) was a jumbled mess of granite boulders.

It was arduous and awkward, a little unnerving, but also satisfying to negotiate a trail that could spank you good if you didn't concentrate. Though we were protected from the wind by the mountain and large boulders we scrambled over, the clouds racing overhead broadcast the conditions on the Knife's Edge, the route we planned to take on the way down.

The summit, just thirteen feet shy of a mile high, was windy and crowded with hikers basking in the glorious view of lakes and ponds and wilderness below. The summit of Katahdin is named after Maine's former Governor Percival Baxter, who purchased 202,064 acres of the surrounding wilderness in the 1920s so that it would remain forever wild. He wrote, "Buildings crumble, monuments decay, wealth vanishes. But Katahdin in all its glory forever shall remain the mountain of the people of Maine."

We were worried about the storm blowing in. We stayed on top just long enough for Nels to take a few dozen photos and headed down the ridge, which reminded me of a crumbled version of the Great Wall of China.

Some people say that if you haven't done the Knife's Edge you haven't climbed Katahdin. That may be an overstatement, but the narrow, mile-long ridge offers enough scrambling and steep, stomach-churning drop-offs on each side to turn a non-climber into a nervous wreck. The scale of the terrain is so deceptively large that trying to find hikers in the distance was like looking for an ant on the back of a dinosaur.

The ridge ends at two rocky pinnacles—the 4,902-foot Chimney Peak and the slightly taller Pamola Peak, which is named after the Indian storm god that regularly lashes this exposed section of the mountain. (Said Thoreau, "Pamola is always angry with those who climb to the summit of Katahdin.")

It took us more than two hours to negotiate the ridge in the steady 20 to 30 mph wind. Once across, we proceeded down the Helen Taylor Trail. A ranger had told us that it was the most gradual (read, easiest) route down. In fact, the 4.3-mile-long trail was relentlessly steep and unforgiving, a brutal assault to the knees. It took us so long to get down that several times we feared we'd wandered off the trail. Our navigation wasn't the problem—it was our undersized expectations. Actually, as an Easterner, I was proud to know such a formidable mountain resided on my side of the Mississippi. At least I would be, once my knees stopped aching. ▲

ALONG THE EAST COAST

- Florida
- Alabama
- Georgia
- South Carolina
- Kentucky
- Pennsylvania
- Maryland
- Delaware

FLORIDA

Britton Hill: *The Lowest of the Low*

Along the East Coast

**Highest Elevation
345 feet**

PEOPLE LOVE EXTREMES. If Denali inspires awe and curiosity, the highpoint of Florida inspires jokes. Tell someone you intentionally visited a spot 345 feet above sea level on a barely noticeable plateau northeast of Paxton, Florida, and he or she will feel compelled to ask if you used oxygen. Those who read *Outside* magazine will ask if you were forced to bivouac overnight.

Located in Lakewood Park in the Florida panhandle near the Alabama state line, Britton Hill enjoys the distinction of being the lowest of America's fifty state highpoints—103 feet lower than the next lowest, Ebright Azimuth in Delaware. To call it less than overwhelming is an understatement: Except for the modest sign proclaiming it Florida's highest point, the 900-by-400-foot plateau off Walton County Road 285 looks like just another roadside picnic area.

Which is not to say it didn't pose any challenges. From the moment we exited the car, it was uphill. We had to negotiate several slick steps, which led to an incline that was clearly more precipitous than a shuffleboard court. *And* it was raining. We had to scuttle at least three dozen yards to the shelter of a pavilion,

which we shared with a condom that lay unfurled on the concrete floor.

Uncomfortable in such unsavory surroundings, we decided to push on to the summit, despite the less-than-ideal weather conditions. The granite highpoint marker was located a solid fifty yards from the pavilion. We walked into a gentle breeze through a small stand of dripping pines. Though our Gore-Tex jackets kept us dry, I stepped in a puddle. If memory serves me correctly, my sock got wet.

I'm not the first writer to take a swipe at Florida's vertically challenged terrain. Describing his trip to the highest point in Miami-Dade County with Jamling Norgay, the son of the first Sherpa to climb Mt. Everest, *Miami Herald* columnist Dave Barry wrote, "We discuss the ascent, and agree that if spoken communication becomes difficult on the summit, we will use hand signals. For example, waving your hand would indicate "Hi!""

When Nels and I arrived at the peaceful spot overlooking a lush field with grazing cattle one day in early March, we'd already climbed more than two dozen highpoints together. Except for Denali, which we'd yet to attempt, and Gannett Peak in Wyoming, where we'd been turned back by a storm near the summit, we'd stood on all the big highpoints west of the Mississippi. In between we'd been to Ecuador and climbed above 18,000 feet on two snow-covered volcanoes. Given the thousands of miles we'd traveled and the heights we'd hit, climbing to the top of Britton Hill had all the glamour of taking an escalator to the second floor of a department store.

Because I have nothing else to write about, at this time I'd like to direct your attention to a few salient facts about the area. Brace yourself.

• Britton Hill was named after Mrs. Hazel Britton, the former postmistress of Lakewood.

• In 1818, General Andrew Jackson and 1,200 soldiers spent three weeks at nearby Lake Jackson (then know as "Big Pond") during his campaign to subdue the Seminole Indians.

• Lake Jackson, which straddles the Florida–Alabama border, is the largest lake in Alabama, but not in Florida.

• The long-leaf yellow pines in the area were purportedly used to make the floors of New York's Waldorf-Astoria Hotel. (Though I've been in the lobby I've never stayed there.)

Did I mention that it rained the entire time we were there?

OK, back to the climb. While Nels searched for an interesting way to photograph the lowest highpoint in America, I headed down the trail that disappeared into the woods. Save for the chattering crickets and raindrops crashing through the dense foliage, it was eerily still.

When I returned to the picnic table, Nels was crouched trying to photograph the condom and the summit monument in the same image. "I'm a dead man," he said. Followed by, "I hate shooting in the rain!"

I ignored his struggles and began reading John Berendt's *Midnight in the Garden of Good and Evil*, which I'd picked up at the airport in Savannah while I was waiting for Nels. Almost immediately I was transported by the weird non-fiction account of isolation and decadence in the historic town of Charleston, South Carolina. At the end of a chapter I looked up to find a fat man smoking a cigarette in a shiny black pickup with JESUS license plates staring at me. Ten minutes later, a gray-haired black man with a pronounced limp stopped by to fill up two huge water jugs from the tap in the parking lot. The rain hammered down on him but he took all the time in the world. A kid on a dirt bike roared back and forth. Cows mooed, crickets chirped, and the rain fell harder.

Three hours later we were still there. At nightfall, Nels turned on the lights in the restrooms by the summit monument. He had me stand just inside the men's room door and shot my darkened profile. This definitely wasn't

Denali. It wasn't even Delaware.

Finally, we loaded up and headed back down the deserted two-lane country road in the dark with our windshield wipers at full tilt. It was still hard to see the oncoming headlights. The moment we crossed into Alabama, thunder roared and bolts of lightning filled the inky black sky. ▲

ALABAMA

Cheaha Mountain: *The Chill of the Deep South*

Along the East Coast

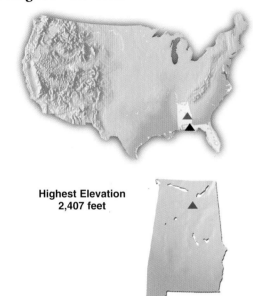

**Highest Elevation
2,407 feet**

SARA MAY, THE MATRONLY WAITRESS at the greasy spoon restaurant in Sylacauga alternated between calling me "honey" and "hon." When she took my order, she asked if I wanted "grits or taters" with my eggs. Every time she sauntered over to our table with the coffee pot, she said, "Y'all want a splash more?"

Much to my dismay, I'd noticed that since we'd been in Alabama southern colloquialisms had started slippin' into my speech. I heard myself saying "Howdy" to gas station attendants. And after we'd paid our bill and Sara May said, "Y'all come back and see us again," I'm sorry to report I said, "We sure will."

As we headed north on Route 21 toward Cheaha Mountain, the 2,407-foot highpoint in the 371,000-acre Talladega National Forest, I asked Nels why Northerners invariably morphed linguistically once south of a certain border (he wouldn't admit it, but he was doing it too). I never noticed the Southerners I ran into on my own turf sounding anything but southern.

"Shoot, I don't know," he said.

After passing through the town of Talladega, the home of the famous

Motor Speedway, we drove the winding scenic road past a handful of graveyards and acres of burnt pines and bare oaks. Back in town—a sunny Sunday in early March—spring was in the air. On the mountain, it was damp and cold. We hurried out of our shorts and into enough layers to go ice fishing.

The stone structure atop Cheaha, built by the Civilian Construction Corps in 1933, looks like a fortress with a weather vane. Next to this medieval-looking edifice is a water tank, a green metal building housing a noisy generator, and a radio tower with high-tech wires. The drone of the generator and hum of the radio wires against the wind added an eerie, industrial feel to the castle-like structure that towered above.

Inside, there was a large puddle on the floor and the sound of water striking stone. Two illuminated soda machines sat against the dark stone wall. Near the top of the metal staircase a garbage can was chained to the handrail. The wind, 30 mph or more, rattled the loosely fit Plexiglas windows in the turret. The graffiti scratched into the plastic bore witness to the many lovers who'd come up for a romantic interlude with a view.

We had the place to ourselves for a while. The 360-degree view—trees and mountains and lakes as far as the eye could see—was splendid if unremarkable. (Cheaha is believed to be the Choctaw Indian word for "high.") On the mountain's southeast slope, future President Andrew Jackson fought against the Creeks in 1813 in a battle called Callabee. In a subsequent skirmish in 1814 he wiped out the entire village at Talladega—part of his campaign that ended in the bloody "Trail of Tears," which forced the tribes in the Creek Nation to relocate west of the Mississippi.

Each section of the country has its own character and feel, but the South, and Alabama in particular, has the most psychological baggage—at least for this New Yorker who had watched the civil rights struggle unfold on television as a child. Partly because the South felt so foreign to me, I took a solo bike trip from Florida to New York a few years ago. Riding through the rural South, I was continually struck by how friendly people were. People with Confederate flags on their lawns invited me to supper; some let me sleep in their homes, even when the home was a school bus on blocks surrounded by junked cars and packs of semi-wild dogs. By the time I got back North, my prejudices had been tempered by first-hand experiences. Another good reason to chase highpoints, if you're looking for a reason.

A slow procession of people trickled through the monument, braving the cold in their short sleeves and shorts. One couple we spoke to had driven from Georgia and stopped by after playing the $21 million Alabama state lottery. Given the frigid weather, all but a few hustled up the tower, hung out for a few minutes, and drove off.

Back on the ground, Nels and I walked down a short embankment and ate lunch on a crag of limestone rock covered with lichen. Farther down the incline, Nels set up his tripod by two charred tree trunks, each as tall as a man. Hunkered down behind the outcropping of limestone, we were out of the wind, in a dense forest of leafless, spindly trees that cut the sunlight into ribbons. When I peered around the rocks, I could see the top half of the monument.

It was a somber, still, and graceful landscape; a place I felt I'd seen before in black-and-white photographs in a tattered old book on the Civil War that my parents owned. There was, of course, no evidence of past bloodshed, just the aimless daydreams of an Eastern mind on Southern soil. ▲

GEORGIA   Brasstown Bald: *One Man's Story*

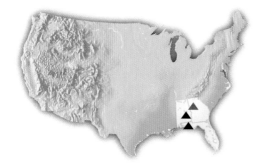

**Highest Elevation
4,784 feet**

TYPICALLY, STORIES OF CLIMBERS and mountains involve a struggle against gravity or weather or altitude. Every once in a while, however, someone makes a mark on a mountain in some way other than a valiant physical conquest or heroic rescue. On Brasstown Bald, the 4,784-foot highpoint located in the north central corner of Georgia in the Southern Appalachians, that man was a dedicated environmentalist named Arthur Woody.

We arrived at the closed visitor center on a Monday morning in early March. The empty parking lot and surrounding trees were coated in ice. We'd planned this southern jaunt to escape the vestiges of a vicious winter still pummeling the Midwest and East. Instead we'd found enough ice in Georgia to do 360s in the parking lot. If it hadn't been so beautiful we'd have been truly pissed off.

We hiked the slick, snowy trail past leafless oak, ash, and maple and huge rhododendron that would bloom in June. According to a trail-side sign, the area to the north and east is a cloud forest, which means that it is usually dripping wet from moisture in the, well, clouds. This environmentally sensitive slope features lichen-covered yellow birch and speckled wildflowers. The area is so verdant that the Cherokee called the summit *itse'yi*, place of fresh green. The first whites confused *itse'yi* with *untsaiyi*, the Indian world for brass; hence the name.

The half-mile uphill walk deposited us in front of a huge, castle-like stone building with a winding staircase that afforded a splendid panoramic view of a sea of mountains with a distinct frost line. The wind whipped the puffy white clouds like floats in a parade. It was a peaceful setting, but there was little to define the place. The drive was pretty but unspectacular. The trail was short and straightforward and no one else was around. I've had more eventful trips to Prospect Park in Brooklyn.

Eventually we were joined by a cheerful couple in their twenties from Peachtree City, Georgia. Admiring our Mountain Hardware Gore-Tex storm shells, the fellow said: "Y'all got real gear; we only got redneck jackets." Though he was shivering, he bounced around like a kid waiting in line to sit in Santa's lap. "We get so excited by snow," he said. "We hardly ever see it."

Nels disappeared to take photographs and I wandered around to the adjacent museum. It was closed, so I peered in the large tinted windows, straining to read the historical tidbits about the area. One sign said that Spaniard Hernando DeSoto arrived here in the 1540s in search of gold. Another mentioned that the Cherokee, who lived in the area as early as 1650, believed that a flood killed everyone save for those who landed on top of the mountain in a great canoe. The Indians were "relocated" in 1828 to accommodate a gold rush that brought a flood of prospectors.

Every few minutes, I did another set of push-ups to warm up.

Staring out one of the windows was a life-sized dummy of a balding, wide-eyed, chubby man with a double chin and goofy smile. It was Arthur Woody, the first Forest Ranger in the Chattahoochee National Forest. I couldn't make out most of what was written so when I got home I surfed the Internet for some information on the good man.

Arthur Woody was born in 1884 in Suches, Georgia, a sleepy town not far from Brasstown Bald. By the turn of the century, man had done a thorough number on Woody's beloved north Georgia woods. Most of the timber had been stripped from the mountains and Woody's father had shot the last deer in the county in 1885. Woody was as intense an activist as any granola-eating tree-hugger you'll meet in the redwood forest. The preservation of his stomping grounds was essential to his sanity. He made false bear tracks to catch poachers and tracked outlaws who hid out in "his" woods. He stocked the creeks of the forest with trout and in 1927 reintroduced deer that he had purchased with his own money. The first stone monument that stood atop Brasstown Bald was conceived, designed, and, with funding by the Federal government, built by Arthur Woody.

I loved the image of Woody hiking the trails barefoot, his trousers unbuttoned and hitched up with suspenders, as he checked on his fish and talked to the game he so fiercely protected. Woody's life took a sad turn in 1941 when the State of Georgia re-opened hunting of the deer he had brought to the woods—many of which he called by name. Seriously depressed by the action, he died in 1946 at the age of sixty-two.

Sitting in New York City, a world away from Georgia's only cloud forest, I thought about Woody gazing out at a sea of green from the monument he originally designed on his kitchen table. More than half a century after his death, Arthur Woody's monument and the woods he loved are grander than ever. ▲

SOUTH CAROLINA Sassafras Mountain: *Be Here Now*

Along the East Coast

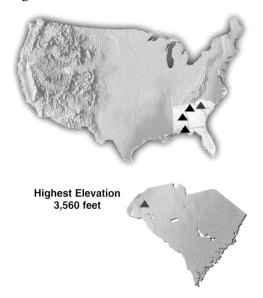

Highest Elevation 3,560 feet

WE MADE OUR WAY FROM Blairsville, Georgia, to Sassafras Mountain in South Carolina like an old country dog picking a spot on the living room rug—winding around and over the Blue Ridge Mountains, through small towns with hand-drawn signs advertising boiled peanuts, and along narrow rivers racing down steep, green hills. For a few hours I enjoyed driving the tight, twisty turns, imagining myself a NASCAR star. But after the stress of passing a dozen logging trucks on a narrow, two-lane road, I couldn't wait to get out of the car and into some sassafras.

Let me say first, that I consider myself an optimist, and second, that I generally try not to let facts get in the way of a good story. But I'm here to tell you that Sassafras Mountain was the most disappointing of the highpoints we'd visited so far.

It didn't help that we couldn't find the turnoff for the highpoint. True, Native Americans call the area "Place of the Lost One," but a sign pointing to the turnoff would have helped. We weren't asking for a neon blinking arrow that said, "Brain-damaged highpointers turn here," although after a five-hour

drive at an average of 24 mph, that would have been most welcome. We'd have settled for an index card tacked to a tree. But there was nothing.

After a handful of fruitless passes, we saw a man on his roof fiddling with his satellite dish and asked directions. He told us that the turn was just after the Camp for the Blind. We noted the irony and impatiently motored 4.7 miles up a paved road to an empty parking lot with huge potholes.

There was an hour left before sunset so we hustled a short distance uphill to the top. Or at least we thought we were at the top. Hard to tell, since there was nothing marking the 3,560-foot highpoint. A large sign surrounded by cigarette butts and beer cans offered information about nearby trails—and a warning about bobcats and rattlesnakes—but it didn't mention that we were on (or near) the top of South Carolina.

The mood felt all wrong, as if we'd showed up a week early to a surprise birthday party. Nels wondered if perhaps the local geological society had found a higher mountain in the state and hadn't told anyone.

The wind was ripping—30 mph or more. It was a good place to fly a kite.

But there wasn't much to sink your highpointing teeth into.

I pushed through a thicket of rhododendrons to a clearing and gazed out over the gently rolling mountains that the Cherokee called "The Great Blue Hills of God." It was pretty, but didn't come close to meeting the expectations nurtured during our endless serpentine drive through the lovely surrounding country.

There have been times when the quest to stand on fifty highpoints—and document the experience—has felt contrived. This was one of them. I looked at the trail map on the sign and realized that what we *should* do was to head down the Foothills Trail to Table Rock State Park, nine miles away. The longest trail in the state winds sixty-five miles along the North Carolina–Georgia border, and takes you past 400-foot cliffs, White Mountain, the largest vertical waterfall drop in the East, and to the Chattooga River, the wild setting for the movie *Deliverance*. Instead, I sat under a tree in the cranking wind and listened to Nels complain about the lack of photo opportunities.

Eventually a near full moon appeared, and by its light I finally found a metal marker embedded in a rock, confirming that we had found the top of South Carolina.

"Hey, Nels, we really are here," I said.

He was busy moving his tripod for the twenty-third time and didn't bother to look my way. "Is that supposed to be a profound metaphysical insight?" he asked.

I thought about that as I dropped to the ground to do a set of push-ups. A highpoint is just a high point, after all. It may be beautiful, it may be interesting, or it may be Sassafras Mountain. I once worked with a fitness trainer who would have me set my watch to beep every hour for one day. When it did, I was supposed to note my posture, breath, attitude—in other words, become aware of myself. Beeper Guru, he called it.

There *is* something arbitrary about visiting highpoints, but maybe that's the point—to bring awareness to wherever you happen to be.

This is probably the perfect time to mention that Sassafras Mountain was named for the sassafras tree. Explorers thought the aromatic bark was a cure-all for disease and shipped it back to Europe. Today it's made into tea, and used to perfume soap and flavor root beer.

When it was too dark to see, we drove slowly down the mountain toward the Camp for the Blind. We turned onto the twisting two-lane road that punishes impatient motorists, and drove toward North Carolina through hills that seemed to go on forever. Assuming we found the next highpoint, we hoped that the view would be a bit better. If it wasn't—well, I could always set my alarm for another round of Beeper Guru. ▲

KENTUCKY

Black Mountain: *A Town Underground*

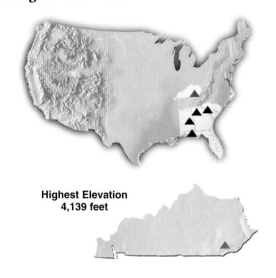

**Highest Elevation
4,139 feet**

METEOROLOGISTS ACROSS THE COUNTRY were calling the impending nor'easter "the storm of the century"— 2 to 200 feet of snow were expected, depending on which hyperbolic forecaster you listened to. It was early March. Nels and I sat over breakfast at a diner outside Asheville, North Carolina, staring at the steady snowfall in disbelief. We dubbed the wacky weather "a colossal pain in the ass."

The Blue Ridge Parkway, our route to North Carolina's Mt. Mitchell, was closed. So was the road leading to Clingmans Dome in Tennessee. The road to Mt. Rogers in Virginia was under eighteen inches of snow and counting. Spruce Knob in West Virginia had had thirty-five inches. Given the miles we had to cover, our allotted time, and scant cold weather gear (who would have thought to bring cross-country skis down South in March?), we felt as if we had driven a convertible into a car wash without putting the top up.

We studied our road atlas and cursed our fate ("this sucks" being the most publishable phrase). We were in southern highpoint heaven and the weather gods were giving us the finger. Climbing all fifty highpoints in America is

enough of a logistical challenge without a freak snowstorm ensuring that we'd have to return to the mountains we couldn't get to.

After a dozen phone calls, and far too much coffee, we headed out to try our luck on the lowest of the four highpoints in the region—Black Mountain in southeastern Kentucky. The wind, 30 mph or more, was blowing the snow sideways. There wasn't much snow on the ground but a whole lot seemed to be on the way. The roads were mostly empty. Except for the trucks and cars with out-of-state license plates, most folks were hunkered down in their homes.

As we climbed higher into the Appalachian Mountains through Tennessee and Virginia into Kentucky, the intensity of the storm picked up. Route 160, a two-lane road that bisects the Virginia–Kentucky state line with more curves than Elizabeth Taylor in her prime, was slick, snow-covered, and buffeted by high winds. As we climbed the switchbacks, I imagined sliding off the road—a dreadful thought given the precipitous drop on one side and jagged rock wall on the other. I later learned that the road is infamous for "cars in the trees."

Black Mountain is not well advertised. To find the turnoff, you need to locate a bullet-riddled sign with the letters FAA. Normally you can drive 1.7 miles up a narrow paved road through the woods that passes the Federal Aviation Administration Long-Range Radar Facility and onto a dirt road to the summit of the 4,139-foot mountain in the heart of coal country. Today, however, was anything but normal.

The side road up Black Mountain had been plowed in. I told Nels to hang on, and I gunned it. The tires slipped as we went from pavement to snow, but we got through. I downshifted and focused hard, fishtailing through some of the larger drifts until the car could go no farther. We'd covered less than fourth-tenths of a mile.

We proceeded on foot. Before long the snow was over our boot tops, with knee-high drifts. The turbulent wind rocked the treetops and produced a sound like waves crashing on the beach.

Hiking a mile-and-a-half uphill in the snow isn't easy, especially without the proper footwear. Still, even headed into the wind, it was far less arduous than scores of snowy climbs we'd done out West. And yet, because we'd assumed we'd motor to the top, amble around the summit and drive down, our snowy slog seemed herculean. Tell someone they have to run five miles and they'll anticipate the end after just two miles. Tell them they've got to run a marathon, and ten miles seems a pittance.

The snow and violent wind and sense of isolation lent an eerie feel to the hike. The scene turned downright surreal when we topped a rise and saw the high-tech FAA facility behind the high-security chainlink fence. I felt as if we'd stumbled on the hideout of the villains in a James Bond movie. Six antennas surrounded a huge, dimpled white ball with thick wires that looked like a cross between a golf ball and a soccer ball.

The summit was a tenth of a mile away. The abandoned lookout tower was riddled with bullet holes. The bottom steps were missing, but if you were willing to shimmy up roughly ten feet of frigid, slippery steel, the rest of the steps appeared intact. We were not willing, and wandered around the bleak summit trying to find something to photograph. The top had all the intrigue of a parking lot.

On the drive down the mountain, we passed through Lynch, a once-thriving coal-mining town that saw its population shrink from 10,000 to less than 2,000 today. There was a ghost-like, slightly creepy feel to this small town sandwiched at the bottom of the steep coal-rich hills. We saw no people as we drove slowly through town. Nothing moved except the snowdrifts blown by the wind. I thought of all the men whose lives were spent underground in the mines, and of the families that had hung on as the town eroded. Talk about alternative realities: We were a couple of mercenary highpointers just passing through, on the rocky start of a ten-day trip that looked to be going nowhere fast. ▲

PENNSYLVANIA Mt. Davis: *A Glimpse of the End*

Along the East Coast

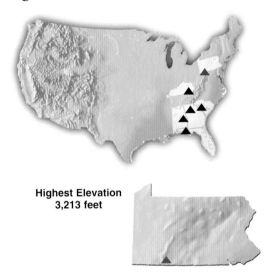

**Highest Elevation
3,213 feet**

AT THE TURN OF THE CENTURY, John Nelson Davis, a Civil War vet turned pioneer farmer, surveyor, teacher, school superintendent, and minister, owned 26,000 acres on Negro Mountain in southwest Pennsylvania. Davis, who was born in 1835, had wide eyes and a feral beard with no mustache. The Negro in question had saved a white family from an Indian attack, dying in the process. Nowhere could I find a name for this brave Samaritan.

In 1921, the U.S. Geological Survey determined that the 3,213-foot Negro Mountain was the highest point in Pennsylvania (3,136-foot Blue Knob had held the honor prior to that), and quickly changed its name to Mt. Davis, eight years after that gentleman's death.

With all due respect to Mr. Davis, as we stood on the modest rise in Pennsylvania Dutch country in early March, it was clear that an IMAX film crew would not be heading this way anytime soon. Yes, we'd had to park nearly two miles from the snowed-in parking lot and walk through a foot of untrammeled snow. And the wind was cranking so hard on top of the open fifty-foot lookout tower (built in 1935 by the Civilian Conservation Corps) that

you had to hold onto the frigid metal railing so as not to be blown off. Still, the most exciting moment of our day had occurred hours earlier, when we passed a bearded Amish man in a horse-drawn buggy.

Physically, Mt. Davis was unremarkable. Historically…well, George Washington had been here in 1753 as a twenty-one-year-old lieutenant. For us, however, reaching the top of Mt. Davis was remarkable because we realized we were finally on the downhill side of our circuitous journey.

Nels and I had climbed our first highpoint in Texas two years earlier, driven thousands of miles together, slept in smelly tents and scores of ratty motels from California to New Hampshire. Side by side, we'd labored under heavy packs, sweated, and shivered. We'd been scared, bored, exhausted, amused, and pissed-off, and still remained solid friends. In fact, not until we'd climbed half of America's highpoints did we fully appreciate the enormity of the task of completing all fifty.

By the time we made it to Mt. Davis, we'd climbed all the big peaks west of the Mississippi except for Denali, and all the highpoints in the northeast.

Our tour down South was truncated by a snowstorm, but we had seen enough below the Mason-Dixon Line to absorb the flavor of that region as well. When we got back to the car after our ascent of Mt. Davis, it seemed the perfect time to reflect on our esoteric tour of America.

Understand that highpointers tend to be serious list-keepers. In fact, the desire to climb all fifty state highpoints may have less to do with the love of mountains than the need to check things off a list. At the halfway point in our trip, we had enough highpoints behind us to indulge in a deeply satisfying session of categorization. Back in the planning stages of the project, we'd roughly divided the highpoints into four basic categories: drive-ups, easy walks, hard hikes, and serious mountaineering challenges. Now we could get much more refined. And waste that much more time.

Nels drove; I turned to a clean page in my notebook. As we headed through the sleepy town of Salisbury en route to Elbright Azimuth in Delaware, we began assembling the high- and low-lights of our journey.

"OK. Tallest, Mt. Whitney; lowest, Britton Hill," I said.

"Could we get a little more obvious, please?" Nels asked. "How about most difficult?"

"Granite Peak," I said, and began writing.

"Whoa! No way! If you take into account the weather, Gannett was clearly more difficult."

This launched a lengthy debate. Montana's Granite Peak was certainly the most technical climb. Although the hand- and footholds are large and obvious, the exposure scared the watery oatmeal out of me. Nels, who'd done a fair bit of rock climbing, found Granite Peak within his comfort zone but had struggled mightily on Gannett Peak in Wyoming. Heading up a steep pitch of ice that led to the summit ridge, he'd had a crisis of confidence, more commonly known in childrearing circles as "wetting his diaper." The blizzard conditions on the way down didn't do much to improve his attitude.

"I'll give Gannett 'Worst Weather' and 'Longest Approach from Trailhead to Summit,'" I said. "But Granite is the more difficult mountain."

"I disagree."

"But I've got the pen."

We also had trouble agreeing on "Worst Argument on a Mountain," since we had had serious tiffs on both Mt. Elbert in Colorado and Kings Peak in Utah, and had fought about money like an old married couple on a long drive through the Sierras. But our progress improved after we broke open a few packs of red licorice. By the time we crossed into Delaware, our list ran to six pages.

"You know that when we finish all fifty, we're going to have to do this all over again," Nels said.

"Great," I replied, and turned over another page. ▲

MARYLAND

Backbone Mountain: *Let There Be Light*

Along the East Coast

**Highest Elevation
3,360 feet**

FOR NEARLY A WEEK in early March, Nels and I endured a spell of foul weather that had settled on the eastern seaboard. What was supposed to be a relaxed tour of southern highpoints—shorts, sandals, shades—had become a slog through snow and rain and wind. Worse, due to road closings we were snowed-out on a handful of mountains, which meant scheduling another trip. Nels seemed particularly bothered. Part of his bad attitude was professional—photographers need sunlight the way a farmer needs rain—but it also seemed as if he'd allowed the weather to influence his mood.

Most of us tend to take the weather personally—a syndrome known as "Why me, why now?" The summer I cycled across America there was a nationwide drought. When I finally got drenched in Ohio, a month into the trip, I was indignant. But a few years back I had a foul-weather breakthrough during a paddling trip in the Adirondacks. I was with a friend named Mike Smith, a farm boy from Michigan I'd met a year earlier on a month-long kayak marathon. On day one of our trip, dark clouds lurked in the distance. Several times—OK, half a dozen—I asked anxiously if he thought it was going to rain.

A tough GM auto worker, Mike once spent a month alone in February camping deep in the Canadian woods where winter is so severe even the moose complain. He finally snapped, "Joe, I quit worrying about the rain a long time ago. I'm going to have a good time either way!"

Wow, what a concept. A weather-proof attitude.

I followed Mike's lead and we had a fine, wet trip. While I still fret about lousy weather, I complain about it a lot less.

Backbone Mountain is located just over the Maryland–West Virginia line in the southwest panhandle of Maryland. At 3,360 feet, the summit is a modest 1.1-mile uphill stroll on a narrow jeep trail through the woods. It earned the name Backbone because of the rocky ridge. The sign on the top calls the summit Hoye Crest in tribute to a veteran of the Spanish-American War and World War I, Captain Charles Edward Hoye, the great-great-grandson of one of the first settlers in the area.

Without the orange letters "HP" spray-painted on the guardrail, the trailhead would be difficult to find. Near the top you pass a weathered concrete monument from 1910 that marks the state line; a neat feature if you're into old, state-line monuments. Put it this way, the hike up Backbone Mountain isn't likely to be one of the highlights of your climbing career. I stood at the top, wishing I could channel the good Captain Hoye and hear a few war stories to help pass the time.

Then the weather gods flipped a switch. And this thoroughly unremarkable day was transformed into a memorable one. For the first time in a week, the sun appeared; the biting wind died. The birds returned. Before you could say melatonin, we were strolling through untrammeled ankle-deep snow like a couple of kids playing hooky from school.

The changes were both obvious and subtle. The sunlight reflected off the snow, turning the woods a brilliant white. The powdery path looked like the world's plushest carpet. Tree limbs swaying in the breeze cast intricate shadows on the sparkling snow. Deer tracks led my eyes off the trail to a buck hiding in a stand of trees. We stood motionless, each watching the other, until the deer bounded off.

Nels, who couldn't stop commenting on the fabulous light, sprawled in the snow with his camera. I sat on a log and watched a fine curtain of snow blow from the trees. As the temperature soared to a balmy 50°F, the snow dropped from bowed branches in clumps and made tiny craters on the trail. Had we been blessed with beautiful weather all week, I might not have noticed these details. I doubt I would have savored them to the point that they acquired the power to transform our modest hike into something special.

We spent an hour at the summit, luxuriating in the sun that streamed through the thicket of trees. I thought back to my two most memorable encounters with weather. One spring I was caught in a blizzard in eastern Montana and ran in place along the banks of the Missouri River for hours to ward off hypothermia. Then, when roughly six months later I managed to get lost in my kayak in a dense fog in Brooklyn's Jamaica Bay and had to spend the night shivering in a downpour, it really didn't seem so bad. It all comes back to the theory of relativity: What's hot to an Inuit is freezing to a Watusi.

Halfway down the trail, the clouds rolled in and covered the sun. The temperature dropped ten degrees in ten minutes. "Hey, Nels," I called, cinching the hood on my jacket. "You about done?" ▲

DELAWARE   Ebright Azimuth: *They Paved Paradise*

Along the East Coast

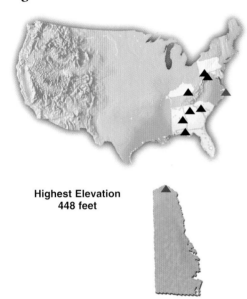

**Highest Elevation
448 feet**

EBRIGHT AZIMUTH—the lone tongue-twister among the fifty state highpoints—stands a non-resounding 448 feet above sea level by the side of a busy two-lane road in front of a modest suburban neighborhood pretentiously named Dartmouth Woods.

It's enough to make you want to drive right on by. And most people do.

We parked at the intersection of Ebright and Ramblewood and walked a few feet to the sturdy sign on the corner stating that we stood atop Delaware—103 feet higher than Britton Hill in Florida. About 100 yards south was a radio tower; across the street was a trailer park and a large empty field.

"Do you see any woods?" I asked Nels.

"No," he replied. "And I don't see any Dartmouths."

We stood staring at the sign, wondering what to do next.

After nearly a week of driving on back roads down South, sitting in morning rush hour traffic on I-95 near Baltimore felt claustrophobic and somehow wrong. When we exited the interstate onto Route 202, we entered a sprawling world of malls, fast-food restaurants, and hotels featuring the names

Brandywine and DuPont.

If our goal was simply to reach Delaware's highpoint, we likely would have lingered for five minutes—or less—in the biting March wind. But we were here to document the place, and the possibilities seemed as limited as a one-way street. Nels photographed the sign from a variety of angles. He complained. He pondered. He despaired.

I stood on the sidewalk feeling like a hungry guy waiting for a table in a crowded restaurant. Some of the residents pulling out of Dartmouth Woods eyed us suspiciously; most were going too fast to notice us.

After an hour, Nels announced, "I want to shoot at night to capture the feel of cars racing by."

It was 10:00 a.m. We could have made it to New Jersey's highpoint that afternoon and been done with our arduous week-long tour. Instead we had eight hours to kill at an intersection in suburban Delaware. While it required less patience than, say, being tent-bound in a storm on Denali, I could think of better things to do with a day.

"Let's get coffee," I said. "You're buying."

We found a Barnes & Noble at a massive mall on Route 202, ordered six bucks worth of Starbucks caffeine, and began browsing. I picked up a copy of *Fast Food Nation* by Eric Schlosser. Subtitled "The Dark Side of the All-American Meal," Schlosser documents how the proliferation of fast food restaurants contributed to the social phenomenon he calls "the malling of our landscape." Given our location—farmland turned strip malls—the book seemed especially relevant.

Throughout our state-by-state tour, it was obvious that no matter how far off the beaten track we got, fast food—and the drive-through culture it supports—was never far behind. Still, until I began reading, I hadn't realized how pervasive it was. As Schlosser points out, fast food is served at airports, zoos, elementary schools, high schools, and universities; on cruise ships, trains, and airplanes; at K-Marts, Wal-Marts, and even hospital cafeterias. If, as Schlosser writes, "A nation's diet can be more revealing than its art or literature," then we're in deep cow manure.

Feeling increasingly bleak, we headed out into traffic to our sign by the side of the road. The marker stated that the elevation of the base of the Ebright Azimuth sign is 448.25 feet. I later learned that a boulder in the nearby trailer park stands slightly higher, at 450.85 feet. However, since the boulder was most likely placed there after the mobile home park was graded, it is considered manmade, and therefore not recognized as the highpoint. Wild stuff, eh?

Clad in a down parka, I walked through the mobile home park to a simple but elegant white stone house on a circular driveway fitted with speed bumps. Two geese sat in front of the house in an open field. Once owned by James and Grant Ebright, the old farmhouse is now an office, less than a quarter mile from the highpoint marker.

While Nels set up his shot on a tripod, I returned to the heated car to thaw out my feet, which felt like blocks of ice. It was 6 p.m.

A few minutes later, a short man with a graying goatee and wild blue eyes stepped out of a white pickup truck. "What are you guys up to?" he asked. He wore a tattered, brown wool hat and camouflage jacket with a Confederate Army pin of crossed guns. His tone was accusatory at best.

When I described our project, he relaxed a bit. For ten years, he said, he'd worked on the horse farm on the Ebright's property. The Ebright house, he said, was built around 1790. Five years ago, he said, the mall with the Barnes & Noble had been Brandywine Race Track. Suddenly, this disconnected landscape—an eighteenth-century stone house surrounded by suburbia—began to make sense.

He left and I went back in the car and continued reading.

By 8:00, Nels returned smiling. "I got a few good shots," he said.

"I'm starving," I said. Nels concurred.

Nine hours after arriving, we headed toward New Jersey, past an assortment of glowing neon signs advertising America's finest fast-food restaurants. ▲

THROUGH THE MIDWEST

- Illinois
- Iowa
- Minnesota
- Wisconsin
- Ohio
- Michigan
- Indiana

ILLINOIS

Charles Mound: *Carefree as a (Wet) Cow*

Through the Midwest

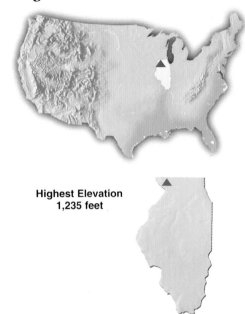

**Highest Elevation
1,235 feet**

ON OCTOBER 10, 2001, two days after the U.S. began bombing Afghanistan, I sat in New York's LaGuardia Airport waiting to board a flight to Chicago. With the threat of a terrorist retaliation on everyone's mind, security was high, the airport eerily empty. Were this a typical Tuesday morning the plane would have been filled with business travelers. Today there were just forty-six people onboard. Presumably I was the only passenger climbing highpoints in the Midwest.

Prior to the September 11 attacks on New York and Washington, the thought of hitting the highpoints in the Midwest—by reputation the least spectacular in the country—interested me about as much as ice fishing. Now I felt anxious about flying and uneasy about my family in New York. But we were all trying to lead normal lives, and for me that meant traveling 900 miles to climb a 1,235-foot "mound."

From O'Hare, I caught a bus to Nels' hometown of Rockford. We stayed up late looking at his slides of the highpoints we'd climbed since we started this project four years ago.

After this round of seven we had ten to go, including the grand finale, Denali, scheduled for the following June.

The next morning, a gray, rainy Wednesday, we picked up two triple caffe lattes, popped in a Dave Matthews CD and headed west and north toward Charles Mound, the forty-fifth-tallest state highpoint in the U.S.

As we drove, I was struck by how, well, Midwestern our surroundings were. We passed a roller rink, fields of pumpkins, and endless rows of desiccated corn stalks. One field had a series of paths cut through its head-high rows. A billboard announced, "Human corn maze."

"That's big out here," Nels said.

"Too bad we can't stop," I replied, trying to sound disappointed.

As we got closer to Wisconsin, we began to see the green and yellow flag of the Green Bay Packers flying outside homes in Lena, Waddams Grove, and Nora. There were plenty of the red-white-and-blue variety as well, but nothing like back home where it seemed as if every car, apartment, and store had suddenly sprouted a flag. For me, the Packer flags were a welcome change, even though I'm a Jets fan.

At the intersection of Stage Coach and East Roberts Road, we crossed a narrow railroad bridge, parked by the side of the road, and hiked down the steep embankment to the slick tracks that disappeared in both directions as far as the eye could see. Back on the bridge, two pairs of silos stood out on the horizon next to a string of telephone wires that vanished alongside the tracks of the Illinois Central Railroad. A green swath of soybeans, the lone splash of color on this otherwise washed-out landscape, was sandwiched between two brown fields of corn. The graceful, undulating lines and sense of space were restful—even comforting, given that the odds of a terrorist attacking nearby Warren (the headquarters of Applejack Cheese) were extremely low.

Charles Mound, one of four state highpoints located on private property, is a short tractor ride from the sleepy farming town of Scales Mound (population 401). According to a notice on the Highpointers Club web site, the owners, Jean and Wayne Wuebbels, require all visitors to get permission before proceeding to the highpoint.

We arrived at noon and stepped out of the rain into the office of Wayne Wuebbels Enterprises. Jean, his wife, was the only one there. She told us they had moved here from Chicago in 1994. "At first I thought I'd lose my mind," she said, "but now I'd never leave." The Wuebbels are only the third owners of the property first settled by Elijah Charles, who lived at the base of the mound.

After getting the go-ahead from Jean, we hustled across the street for lunch at Jake's Place, a smoky bar-and-grill with a large wood bar, graffiti on the ceilings, and plenty of beer-drinking farmers laughing and talking about farming.

We drove to the locked gate outside the Wuebbels' gravel driveway, parked, and started sidestepping puddles in the rain. The fall foliage was peaking and it was good to walk after sitting around all day. Mrs. Wuebbels told us that they get "several hundred" visitors each year, but we were all alone, save for a dozen cows grazing behind a barbwire fence 100 yards away. I shouted, "Hello!" A hefty male, apparently the leader, jogged down the hill to check us out. Given his sociable nature, I continued my one-sided monologue. He moved ever closer, until he nearly touched Nels' large lens with his prodigious tongue. As wildlife encounters go on Charles Mound, it was high drama.

The relaxing mile-and-a-half walk was about as modest as the decor at Jake's Place. There was a stand marking the highpoint and another with a hospitable greeting from the Wuebbels. Two lawn chairs under two small trees sat on either side of a metal milk box with a rock on top and a summit register inside.

I stood in the rain looking out toward Wisconsin. Large, dark clouds raced by. Soon window-shaking thunder claps sounded, the wind picked up, and the rain fell far harder. I stood in my waterproof jacket beneath one of the leafless trees. My feet were freezing and my shorts were soaked. Still, we didn't seem to be hurrying back to the car. Fires were burning in lower Manhattan; bombs were exploding in Afghanistan. Charles Mound, even in the rain, seemed like a fine place to be. ▲

IOWA

Hawkeye Hill: *America's Welcome Center*

Through the Midwest

**Highest Elevation
1,670 feet**

WE CROSSED THE MISSISSIPPI in Dubuque, near the farm where the movie *Field of Dreams* was filmed, and headed west across Iowa on state roads as straight as a rake handle, through sleepy towns like Hayfield and Cylinder, Melvin and Cloverdale. We saw lots of grain silos, churches, bare brown fields, and shiny farm machinery for sale.

It's exciting country if you're in the market for a thresher, but if you're searching for a vertical experience that doesn't involve a grain elevator, there is not a whole heck of a lot to sink your crampons into. In *Great Plains*, Ian Frazier wrote, "America is like a wave of higher and higher frequency toward each end, and lowest frequency in the middle." Had north-central Iowa been hooked up to an EKG machine, the line would have had nary a wobble.

The next morning we had breakfast in Sibley, a town of 2,000 with cobblestone streets and old-fashioned lampposts, named after General Henry

Hastings Sibley, an Indian fighter who became the first territorial governor of Minnesota. From Sibley, we headed north on Route 60, turned right on a gravel road, and proceeded 0.2 mile up the road toward a tower that read "Osceola Rural Water."

The first farm house on the right belongs to Merrill and Donna Sterler. We turned into the second of their two driveways, parked, and walked seventy-five yards toward a feed trough. Before you could say *The Sibley Gazette Tribune* six times slowly, we were there—1,190 feet higher than Iowa's lowest point. One must ascend a full ten vertical feet to reach the top. Toddlers and people with severe soybean allergies should take care. And regardless of your fitness or experience as a mountaineer, you need to be on alert for cyclones.

It's hard to take Hawkeye Hill too seriously, considering that no one even bothered to name it until 1998. In *Fifty State Summits*, it goes by the generic name "High Point." In *Highpoints of the United States*, it's listed as "Unnamed."

Prior to the 1971 U.S. Geological Survey, Iowa's highpoint was thought to be Ocheyedan Mound, which was once used by Indians as an observation point and by settlers as a beacon to cross the prairie. Though more prominent and picturesque, Ocheyedan Mound turned out to be fifty-seven feet lower. Iowa has the distinction of being the last state to officially name its actual highpoint.

We arrived on a clear, sunny Thursday morning in early October. No one seemed to be home at the Sterler's and there were no visitors milling about on the manicured lawn. The highpoint is alongside an old feed trough with a roof—a fitting monument given its surroundings.

Attached at the end of the trough's roof was a sign in the shape of Iowa inscribed with "Hawkeye Point, elevation 1,670 feet." Below were seven license plates: including two from Alaska ("The Last Frontier") and one from Delaware ("The First State"). There was a summit log in a metal box with Iowa-shaped plastic key chains (free) and a baseball cap with the Hawkeye Hill logo for sale at $7 per cap (honor system).

According to the summit register, we were the fifth party to visit in the last eleven days. In July, someone had written that the corn, which was now broken, dried stalks scattered on the ground, was "as high as an elephant's eye." A few entries later, a woman wrote that this was the first highpoint she'd visited since her husband died three months earlier. "Michael taught me how to see the beauty in everything," she wrote, "and the joy of highpointing. I do this highpoint in his memory."

That got me thinking about my mom, who'd died a year before. The scene was so unremarkable, so quintessentially American, I suspected she'd have had little patience with it. My mom was the ultimate city hound (someone who soaked up culture by the gallon). The Sterler's white house had a basketball hoop, bird feeder, and large silver dinner bell near a satellite dish. There was a weathered red barn with broken window panes, a grain silo, and a swing set that looked as if it hadn't been used in a few seasons. The sky was bright blue and cloudless; the wind strong enough to send a kite soaring over the state line 2.9 miles north.

I leaned against the barn. Shielded from the wind, I gazed out across a fallow field bathed by the sun. It was so unlike the frenetic city I call home and so different from the hip mountain towns like Missoula, Montana, or Telluride, Colorado, that I think about moving to. But as Ian Frazier wrote, "The beauty of the plains is not just in themselves but in the sky, in what you think when you look at them, and in what they are not."

Hawkeye Hill may not have the historical significance of Ocheyedan Mound, or the romance of Madison County, or of that other Iowa cornfield where Kevin Costner conjured up Shoeless Joe Jackson. But if you hang out on the Sterler's farm long enough and allow the stillness, space, and sun to envelope you, the land may inspire you in ways you never imagined. ▲

MINNESOTA

Eagle Mountain: *By the Shores of Gitchee Gumee*

**Highest Elevation
2,301 feet**

AS WE PASSED THROUGH Knife River, a small town along Lake Superior, Nels pointed to a shimmering ray of light in the distance. "What the hell?" he asked. According to the map, Grand Marais, the only town of consequence, was a hundred miles away. I guessed that it might be a search light from a local airport or prison. As we drove north along Highway 61, the streaks of light multiplied, then brightened. Thirty minutes later, with Billy Joel's "Piano Man" blasting from the radio, a fluffy, bright-white curtain covered half the sky.

"It's the northern lights," Nels announced. "Aurora borealis."

I'd seen plenty of photos of this celestial phenomenon but never the real thing. Seven hours after leaving Iowa's Hawkeye Hill, we'd long since entered the road-weary stage, twitchy-legged and over-tired, unable to think of anything but getting out of the car. Stumbling upon this extravagant light show perked us up as if we'd seen a rainbow for the first time.

Nels had been here a year earlier and knew a place where we could get an unobstructed view over the lake. It was nearly 11 p.m. when we turned onto a narrow, twisting road that climbed to a spot called Palisades Lookout. Using a flashlight powerful enough to guide a spaceship to a parking space, Nels led us down the rocky incline. "Be careful," he warned, shining his light toward a sheer rock wall that fell hundreds of feet into Lake Superior. "If you fall, you die!"

Enough said.

When we could walk no farther, he turned off the light. The wispy luminescent streaks reminded me of the spiked hair of a Smurf doll. Streamers of pink and green and gray frolicked through the smoky curtain of light in a sky filled with stars. We stared above in awe, serenaded by the waves crashing against the cliff. We were a long way from the windy Iowa farm we'd visited earlier in the day, and not just in miles.

Located in the Boundary Waters Canoe Area Wilderness of Superior National Forest, Eagle Mountain is the northern-most highpoint in the 48 contiguous states. The highest point in the land of 10,000 lakes stands just 2,301 feet, but the wilderness in which it resides is the largest national forest outside of Alaska and one of the greatest wilderness waterways in the world.

In other words, Eagle Mountain presides over an area with big medicine. Superior National Forest has 445,000 acres (635 square miles) of surface water. There are some 1,500 miles of canoe routes, more than 1,000 lakes and streams and more bogs than a Scotsman could shake a stick at. (According to native son Garrison Keillor, Lake Woebegone was mistakenly left off the Minnesota state map.) Superior National Forest is also the last stronghold in the Lower 48 of the endangered timber wolf. This dense boreal forest—filled with fir, spruce, aspen, and birch—is also home to moose, bear, and the common loon. (The loon is the state bird, although the mosquito has the unofficial title.) This combination of water, rock, and forest comprises a wilderness so vast it boggles the mind. Minnesota may be mostly flat, but hiking up Eagle Mountain is far from a casual stroll around another Midwestern cornfield.

In the morning we continued toward Grand Marais along Lake Superior's western shore. The first Frenchmen, who came via the Ottawa River and Lake Huron, called it *le lac superieur*, or the Upper Lake. The Chippewa Indian translation, *Gitchi gummi*, means Great Water. English poet Henry Wadsworth Longfellow called it the "Shining Big-Sea-Water." By any name, with 2,800 miles of shoreline it looks so much like an ocean that it was hard not to think we'd gone terribly wrong and ended up in Maine overlooking the Atlantic.

Nels and I have paddled hundreds of miles on Lakes Michigan, Ontario, and Erie, and I'm here to say those lakes are freakin' huge. Yet those three, plus Huron, plus three more the size of Erie, could fit inside Lake Superior. With a maximum depth of 1,333 feet, water cold enough in the middle of summer to paralyze a capsized boater in less than ten minutes, and winter storms that swallow ocean liners whole (remember Gordon Lightfoot's "The Wreck of the Edmund Fitzgerald"?), Superior is a name well deserved.

One of the peculiarities of travel is that when you go out of your way to visit a place—even briefly—it becomes yours. During the drive, we waxed poetic about the greatest of the Great Lakes like a Jewish mother bragging about her son the doctor.

This massive body of water only begins to make sense when you learn a bit about the forces that shaped it. When the last Ice Age rumbled through roughly 12,000 years ago, it created a landscape of low, rounded mountains and bare rocky outcroppings. When the glacier melted, well, it left one hell of a big puddle. Many of Minnesota's countless lakes tumble from the Sawtooth Mountains—the pinnacle being Eagle Mountain—to the lowest point in the state, the shores of Lake Superior. Wadsworth wrote in *The Song of Hiawatha*, "On its margin the great forest stood reflected in the water."

Oh yes, the hike. The trailhead for the Eagle Mountain Trail begins at a dirt parking lot in a forest filled with white pine, spruce, aspen, and fir. The first half of the 3.5-mile walk is a narrow, flat, rocky trail through dense forest—relaxing rather than scenic. At Whale Lake, a pristine body of water that served as a perfect foreground to Eagle Mountain, we followed a turnoff to the left and headed up the mostly rocky trail to a metal plaque on a boulder that marks the summit.

It had been a thoroughly satisfying, if unspectacular, walk in the woods.

The spot didn't feel much like a summit—just a clearing in the woods with a view of Lake Superior and the Boundary Waters Canoe Area Wilderness surrounded by a forest just past peak foliage. The silver glint of water was everywhere in the endless landscape. I realized, with great pleasure, that most of it drained into Lake Superior—my lake—the biggest and grandest you'd ever hope to see. ▲

WISCONSIN

Timms Hill: *In the Heart of Akerlund Country*

Through the Midwest

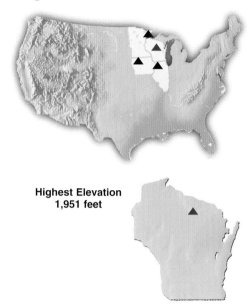

**Highest Elevation
1,951 feet**

NELS AND I HAD JUST SPENT three days holed up in his office in Rockford writing photo captions for a book we'd collaborated on about the Wisconsin River. He'd dedicated nearly three years to the project, paddling the 427-mile river end-to-end and returning many times to capture the river's different moods. I'd spent a week paddling the river's scenic sections and written the text. Writing the captions was our final task before the book was put to bed.

We finished late on a Sunday night, plopped down in his living room, beers in hand. Before I could say "Cheers!" Nels blurted out, "I've got another idea!"

I was hoping his idea was to rent a video and order a pepperoni pizza, but I knew better.

Nels has an entrepreneur's head and adventurer's soul; he's a workaholic who gets bored easily. He does commercial and architectural photography, designs web sites, and often works late at night welding scrap metal into funky furniture (which he sells at a handsome profit). When he's not photographing aerosol cheese, lawn furniture, or the Wisconsin State Capitol, he's thinking up highly non-commercial ideas that will take him far from the familiar confines of

Rockford, the town in which he was born and raised. When the phone rings late at night, it's usually Nels asking if I want to sail around the world, make a pilgrimage to Mecca, or do a book on Jewish cemeteries in Poland.

I braced for the inevitable.

"Let's do a book on the highest mountain in each of the fifty states."

I said no.

He told me why we should.

I told him I'd spent too much time and made too little money on our last gig to get involved in something so time-consuming.

That was in December 1997. Four months later, we climbed Guadalupe Peak in west Texas. And four years later, on a rainy morning in October, we were back in Wisconsin en route to Timms Hill, highpoint number thirty-eight. Seeing the river again, it seemed as if we'd come full circle. In 1997, we'd launched our kayaks at the headwaters at Lac Vieux Desert and paddled forty serpentine miles in the rain to Eagle River, where we'd spent the night in a quaint cabin owned by Nels' uncle. As a boy, Nels spent weeks in Eagle River each summer fishing with his family. During high school, when he wanted to get away, he'd grab his camera and head north to explore different parts of the river. And a time-honored tradition in Nels' family was the annual fall fishing trip.

In fact, when we pulled into Eagle River at noon, a dozen men of the Akerlund clan were out on some lake nearby, drinking coffee and fishing in the rain. Had we arrived later, we would have joined the muskie-eating mob for dinner. But we had other fish to fry. Nels left a message for his dad and we drove south and west toward Timms Hill, the 1,951-foot highpoint located five miles east of Ogema.

Timms Hill and Timms Lake (not to be confused with Bass Lake across the road) were named after Timothy Gahan, who logged white pine, hemlock, and hardwood in these woods at the turn of the century. His sawmill on the east side of Bass Lake closed in 1907. Timms Hill was last logged in 1944. Price County bought 187 acres around the highpoint in 1978; it's been a park ever since.

Timms Hill County Park is a peaceful place with a parking lot, pavilion, and playground for kids. It was raining lightly when we arrived at 3:00 on a Saturday afternoon. We walked 0.2 mile up a trail covered with leaves to the deserted observation tower. Eighty-eight steps later, we were treated to an expansive view: six lakes set between rolling hills bathed in fall colors. Patches of fog nestled between the evergreens in a tree farm. Dislodged by the rain and buffeted by the strong wind, the sky was littered with leaves fluttering to the ground like tiny multi-colored parachutes.

Nels went down to take photos and I stood in the tower alone, feeling like a sentry. I stood on my windy perch for over an hour. I watched the floating leaves and listened to the wind as Nels bustled about below. For Nels, Wisconsin was a place that defined his childhood and occupied much of his time as a photographer. His roots were firmly in the Midwest; mine were embedded in the concrete back East.

Years ago, when he told me that he ate breakfast at the Swedish Pancake House every Wednesday with his father, uncles, brother, and his ninety-three-year-old grandfather (Nels Sr.), I thought, "How hokey." And then I realized that I was jealous. Being so comfortable and familiar with his surroundings and within his tight-knit family may explain why he was so confident and eager to explore the world. He was compelled to leave, in part, because it was so familiar. But when he returned he enjoyed a sense of belonging that I did not have, growing up in an unceremonious family of skeptical intellectuals who had little relationship with the land we lived on and a tenuous relationship with our own cultural heritage.

This fall Nels missed the fishing trip to Eagle River because we were out climbing highpoints. But next year, if he's around, he'll be back, catching muskies, drinking beer, and telling the same bad jokes that were told the year before. Standing in a windy tower at the top of the state, I gazed over the horizon and pondered the paths that had led each of us to Timms Hill on a quiet, rainy day in October. ▲

OHIO Campbell Hill: *Hi Pointing Monday thru Friday*

Through the Midwest

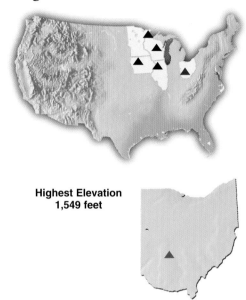

**Highest Elevation
1,549 feet**

IF YOU HAPPEN TO ARRIVE in Bellefontaine, Ohio, late at night in search of lodging, you may want to consider bypassing the Mountaintop Motel. We'd read that Campbell Hill was a visual snooze and Nels hoped that the motel at night would provide a photo op. We arrived around 10:30 p.m. The parking lot was filled with construction vehicles and the sidewalk in front of the motel was dug up. We were stupefied from the long drive, and the room's concrete walls and tattered, dark-green wall-to-wall carpeting greeted us like a surly bouncer. The reception on the TV stunk, the beds were as lumpy as a pug's face and the room smelled like an ashtray. At $75 per night, it was far from a bargain.

Nels exhaled loudly. Clearly he had hoped for something a bit more alpine-lodgishy. Or at least a better color scheme.

Nels headed out to the parking lot to shoot the neon-lit Mountaintop Motel sign. It was midnight when he returned. Though his attitude had improved, he wasn't likely to be confused with Prince Charming. "I got a few halfway decent shots," he said.

It was not one of our more auspicious starts.

Located two miles outside of Bellefontaine, Campbell Hill had been known as "Hogue's Hills" until Charles D. Campbell purchased the property in 1898. A beer magnate named August Wagner next bought the land, and his daughter later deeded it to the federal government in 1950. The 1,549-foot highpoint had been home to an Air Force radar station until 1969. The Ohio Hi-Point Joint Vocational School set up shop there in 1974.

We headed up Route 540 and turned right into the fenced facility that is only open during the week. We drove toward a flagpole and walked fifty yards up a hill to a small brick concourse and a white stone marked with an X. The wind pulled the flag tight; birds of prey soared above the manicured lawn that dropped off in front of us. Had there been snow, it would have been a perfect hill for sledding.

It was 9 a.m. on a Monday in October. Although the parking lot below was busy with students and teachers headed to class, things were kind of slow on this windy spot at the top of Ohio. A radio antenna and large blue tower with "Aqua Store Tank System" painted on it stood behind us. The rolling hills before us were bright with fall colors.

"It's a big field of nothing," said Nels.

I informed him that we had a great view of the Cosmetology School and the Animal Care Facility.

Nels responded with, "I should have brought my dog. He could have had a makeover and a place to stay."

Even our vocational school humor seemed flat.

An hour later, at 11 a.m., Nels announced that he could shoot no more. We'd gone to bed without eating dinner (no all-night diners in Bellefontaine) so we headed back to town in search of breakfast.

Just outside the fenced complex, we passed a small brick box-like building behind a chainlink fence—the Hi Point Church of Christ. Nels had me pull over so he could photograph it. (I'm not sure if the spelling of "high" was meant to be phonetic or folksy, but it was all over town.) The shot promised to be as exciting as the pile of dirt in the parking lot of the Mountaintop Motel.

A few minutes later, we drove downtown. Canary-yellow flags inscribed with "Peak of Ohio" lined both sides of Main Street. Considering that Campbell Hill ranked forty-third in height, it seemed odd that Bellefontaine was so eager to celebrate its status in the Buckeye State.

"Pull over," Nels said. He wanted to photograph the flags. We parked at the intersection of Main and Court. As he walked up and down the street snapping away, I read a sign outside the Court House that informed me that I was standing on the first concrete street in America. In 1891 an eight-foot strip was built here to hitch horses. Two years later, Court Avenue was paved and history was made.

Nels returned with a grin on his face. "I got some decent shots," he said. It was well past noon and I was famished.

We drove through traffic on South Main Street looking for a place to eat. Much to my horror, Nels shouted, "Turn here!" He pointed up at a huge sign ushering vehicles into a parking lot. The profile of a snow-covered mountain, highlighted by a brilliant red sunset, towered over a sprawling shopping complex. The mountain looked like Mt. Hood. Beneath the image, in bold letters, it read, HIGHPOINT VILLAGE. Below that, Wal*Mart.

Nels shouted again, "We've found the mother lode!"

We parked near a Taco Bell. People in cars heading into and out of the parking lot stared as Nels worked around the sign.

But it was nearly 2:00 before Nels was finished, and we were too impatient to get back in the car to search for a Mom 'n' Pop restaurant. Instead we ran across the street to Bob Evans. We sat by the window and dined on pre-fab family-style cooking with a perfect view of the Highpoint Village sign. I comforted myself that at least we'd not spent the night in a franchise. The Mountaintop Motel may have had a few kinks to iron out, but at least it had character and was far more memorable than a Motel 6. ▲

MICHIGAN

Mt. Arvon: *The Snowshoe Priest of Baraga County*

Through the Midwest

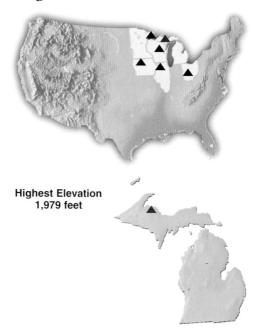

**Highest Elevation
1,979 feet**

GEOGRAPHICALLY, Michigan has a split personality. Surrounded by Lakes Michigan and Huron, the Lower Peninsula lies like a tattered mitten, bordered on the south by Ohio and Indiana. The Upper Peninsula, separated from its lower half by a narrow waterway called the Straits of Mackinac, is bordered on the southwest by Wisconsin and joins Ontario, Canada, far to the east. Before the five-mile-long Mackinac Bridge was finished in 1957, you had to drive hundreds of miles along the west shore of Lake Michigan to get from one peninsula to the other.

Mt. Arvon, Michigan's highpoint, is located near the southern end of Lake Superior's Keweenaw Bay. Eagle Mountain, where we started our drive in northern Minnesota, presides over the west side of Gitchee Gumee. It was a short flight as the crow flies, but by car, a nine-hour drive through three states.

Logic would seem to dictate that the Upper Peninsula, which adjoins Wisconsin, would be part of the Badger State. But it was a dispute between

Michigan and Ohio in 1837—over a strip of land along their border that included Toledo—that gave the Wolverine State its peculiar shape. Ohio won, and as compensation Congress gave Michigan statehood and the western two-thirds of the Upper Peninsula. What seemed like a bum deal for Michigan at the time turned out to be a bonanza in terms of natural resources like copper and iron ore.

The drive seemed to take forever. At midnight we arrived in L'Anse (rhymes with dance), a small town fifteen miles east of Mt. Arvon. We were so tired we found a motel and hit the hay without eating dinner.

L'Anse bills itself as "The Village by the Bay." Michigan natives Henry Ford, Francis Ford Coppola, and Madonna may be more famous out of state, but when we hit the Hilltop Restaurant for breakfast the next morning it was apparent that the biggest name in town was Frederic Baraga, the first Bishop of the Upper Peninsula. We saw a framed photo of a sixty-foot copper statue of the Bishop holding a seven-foot cross in one hand and a pair of snowshoes twenty-six-feet-long in the other. The Slovenian traveled first to Canada, arriving in Michigan in 1830. He befriended the Chippewa, learned to speak their language, and founded five Catholic missions along the south shore of Lake Superior. One winter he walked more than 700 miles on his snowshoes to serve his churches, hence his nickname "The Snowshoe Priest." The last of his missions was located in L'Anse, where he presided from 1843 to 1853.

Michigan's highpoint had the reputation of being the hardest of any to find—due to logging in the area, the roads around Mt. Arvon changed more frequently than a chorus girl in a Broadway show. Mercifully, a few years ago a series of blue-and-white diamond-shaped signs marking the route were set up along Ravine River Road, and now the trailhead is virtually impossible to miss.

Prior to 1963, Porcupine Mountain in the northwest part of the state was thought to be the highpoint. Next, the USGS identified Mt. Curwood as the granddaddy. But in 1982 a USGS survey revealed that at 1,979 feet Mt. Arvon was nearly a foot taller. While the new measurement was news in Baraga County, the revelation hardly shook up the mountaineering world.

The gradual mile-long hike on a rutted old logging road gained a modest 300 feet to the top. In a small clearing in the woods highlighted by scores of birch, we stood in the rain in front of a mailbox that sported a diamond-shaped sign that congratulated us for reaching Michigan's highest point.

Although the trees were at peak colors there was no view. The wind rocked the treetops with a dull roar. Two blue benches in the clearing seemed strangely out of place, as did a pile of chopped wood with a half-full bottle of Boone's Farm Snow Creek Berry wine.

Before the attacks on September 11, many of the people who wrote in the summit register housed in the mailbox were nearly contemptuous of Mt. Arvon's modest vistas. "This was the most boring highpoint to date," wrote a guy who'd been to thirty-one. "This view stinks," wrote a resident of Fox Lake, Illinois. "What a waste of time," scrawled another disgruntled hiker.

After the attacks, the tone of the entries changed dramatically. "I'm saying a prayer for the lost ones," or "God Bless America," were typical. Others used positive adjectives to describe the summit like "quiet," "humble," and "quirky." Interesting to see how an event can change people's perception of a neutral surrounding. I returned to a bench and flashed back to where I'd been a month and two days earlier on that beautiful Tuesday morning.

The madness of that day and sense of doom that had permeated New York City since then seemed distant on a soggy blue bench in a wooded clearing atop Michigan. I picked up the bottle of Boone's Farm "flavored apple wine product," opened the twist-off cap and thought about taking a swig. But even an unopened bottle of Boone's Farm is suspect, so I put the cap back and mentally toasted the serenity of the quiet, crappy view. ▲

INDIANA Hoosier Hill: *High-Stile Highpointing*

Through the Midwest

**Highest Elevation
1,257 feet**

"WHAT'S A HOOSIER?" I asked Nels, as we sped across the Indiana state line just west of Fort Recovery, Ohio.

"It's a basketball player from Indiana," he said earnestly.

I flashed him an "Are you kidding me?" look.

"Larry Bird is from French Lick, Indiana. He's a Hoosier."

"But what is it?"

"A film starring Gene Hackman."

"You have no idea, do you?"

I had thought everyone except me knew what a Hoosier was. Only later did I learn that the question has challenged historians for years. The term came into general usage in the 1830s when John Finley of Richmond wrote a poem, "The Hoosier's Nest," which appeared in the *Indianapolis Journal*, January 1, 1833. The image of a Hoosier roosting deepened my confusion, and I continued my research. One theory suggests it derived from "Who's yere?"—the typical response to a knock on an Indiana pioneer's door.

Some say that there once was a contractor on the Louisville & Portland Canal named Hoosier who would only hire workers from Indiana, hence the term "Hoosier's men." Historian Jacob Piatt Dunn traced the word back to "hoozer," in the Cumberland dialect of England, which derives from the Anglo-Saxon word "hoo" meaning high or hill. Dunn says that Hoosier was used down South in the nineteenth century to refer to rough hill people.

By any definition, there were precious few Hoosiers on this desolate field of cornhusks when we arrived on a raw, windy Tuesday morning in October. The 1,257-foot highpoint, which is on the property of Kim Goble, is tucked in the woods on a small rise off Elliot Road, northwest of Bethel in Wayne County.

We parked by the side of the straight and narrow two-lane road, disturbing two turkey buzzards that picked at a dead raccoon in the rain. We walked about fifty feet through a field, turned right at a pile of two dozen car tires, and faced a grove of trees blocked by a barbwire fence.

The crux of the climb is the stile, five steel steps with a handrail, that takes you up, over, and down the fence into a small clearing in the woods. (The stile was donated by the Highpointers Club in 1991.) Two benches were chained to

112

trees on opposite ends of the small clearing littered with leaves. Each offered a good—though remarkably similar—view of the sign that stood behind a rather incongruous pile of stones. It read, "Indiana's Highest Point." A small American flag, no doubt placed there after the events of September 11, was taped on the right side of the sign.

Looking out over the stile, a red barn in the distance stood out as the lone splotch of color in the barren field. While the wind was blowing hard outside, inside the damp clearing it was relatively still. If you had a good book or were fond of meditation, this was the place for you. However, on a cold, damp day, it was on the wrong side of uneventful. Nels had his work cut out for him in this modest clearing in the woods.

I sat looking out the window of the car, thinking back to the summer I crossed Indiana by bike. Before I started my cross-country trip people warned me I'd be bored to tears by the Midwest's monotonous landscape. After crossing the Rockies, almost any landscape would seem dull, but by the time I got to Indiana I was pleasantly surprised by how much I enjoyed riding on the empty country roads that bisected fields of tall corn en route to towns that seemed straight out of a Norman Rockwell painting. One of the most memorable experiences of my forty-four-day ride occurred near Hoosier Hill.

After riding more than 100 miles one warm August day, I fell asleep at dusk behind the pavilion at a municipal pool near Kokomo. At 2 a.m. I was wide awake with no place to go. It was clear and windless, so I packed up and began riding east into the night on Route 26, a road as straight as a rake handle.

All was quiet save for the sound of crickets and my tires racing along the smooth pavement. Initially I was anxious; however, energized by the cool air and excitement of riding at night, I rode over the undulating terrain so effortlessly I felt as if I were flying. Every five or ten or fifteen miles, I'd spot the glow of the flashing traffic light in the center of town, blinking for no one. I'd ease up at the crossroad, peering in the storefront windows for clues about the people who lived in the sleepy surroundings.

By sunrise I'd ridden fifty miles. At 6:00 a.m. I stood outside a diner waiting for the waitress to open up. Half an hour later, I sat in the corner wolfing eggs and pancakes and swilling coffee as families in their Sunday finest greeted each other like frat brothers. After my magical nighttime ride I felt as spiritually uplifted as any church-goer in the state.

The memory reminded me of the saying, "God is in the details." When I returned to the clearing, Nels stood behind his tripod shooting rusted barbwire that had become embedded in the bark of the tree.

"Seen any Hoosiers?" I asked.

"It's too cold."

I made another bad joke but Nels was absorbed by the rusty wire. "I'm trying to find a way to capture the tranquility of this place."

A long time passed before he moved to the other side of the clearing. This time he set up his tripod in front of two leaves hanging precariously from a branch. I sat on the opposite bench and watched them flutter in the wind like the wings of a monarch butterfly. When we returned to the car half an hour later it was raining again. The buzzards were still picking away at the raccoon by the side of the road. ▲

A SOUTHERN TOUR

- Missouri
- Arkansas
- Louisiana
- Mississippi
- West Virginia
- North Carolina
- Virginia
- Tennessee

MISSOURI
Taum Sauk Mountain: *Center of the Highpointing Universe*

A Southern Tour

**Highest Elevation
1,772 feet**

JACK LONGACRE lives alone on fifty acres of woods in a double-wide trailer at the end of a long driveway two-and-a-half miles from Taum Sauk Mountain. The seventh person to climb all fifty highpoints (he's soloed all but Denali and Rainier), he's stood atop thirty-nine of them a second time. Even before we met it was clear that the sixty-four-year-old founder of the Highpointers Club is not your average senior citizen.

Driving down Country Road CC, a two-lane road that winds through the Ozarks past trailers with car parts piled around them, we turned down a gravel driveway at a sign welcoming "all hikers and highpointers." A second sign read "Speed Limit 7.3 mph." Farther on are two mounds of earth that look like gravesites. One says, "RIP, Here Rests Lady Litterbug." The other, with a plastic bunny in front, warns, "Kaution: Jakkrabbit Krossing." And outside his narrow wood porch (where he sleeps in the nude on sultry summer nights) is a post with arrows pointing to fifteen highpoints across the country. Mt. Whitney is 1,004 miles away; Mt. Marcy, 985.

We arrived on a cold, windy Friday morning in February. Longacre's tidy four-room home is a shrine to the great outdoors: There's a collection of gnarled walking sticks by the front door; over his bed, a dream-catcher with stones and broken arrowheads he found out West; and a statue of a wolf, his alter ego, on the TV. Above the couch is a framed plaque honoring ten years of outstanding service to the Highpointers Club. An entire wall in his cramped office is filled with cases of the newsletter he penned in longhand from 1987 until 1998, when he handed the reins of the club to John Mitchler and Dave Covill in Colorado.

The morning we showed up, Jack was scheduled to go for his ninth chemotherapy treatment to combat Hodgkin's disease. But while Nels took photographs outside, Jack took time to sit with me at his kitchen table and talk.

I learned that for the first thirty-eight years of his life, he climbed no higher than the ladder he used to clean his gutters.

After his marriage of twenty-three years ended, he moved to Seattle in 1978 to work for Boeing. Staring at Mt. Rainier every day, he thought, "Hey, I'm from Michigan, I'm going to put me on some galoshes and a hunting coat and just trundle on up." When he was told that without proper training he had a snowball's chance in a jet factory of making it to the top, he signed up for a class with Boeing's climbing club. His first jaunt was to the top of Mt. Hood. Rainier followed—"without guides!" he announced proudly.

And so a hard-core highpointer was born. Jack read Frank Ashley's *Highpoints of the United States*, realized he'd completed two of the most difficult, and began bagging other western highpoints—and lots more in between. (He climbed every peak in the Cascades' Tatoosh range as well as one mountain in Washington for every letter of the alphabet.) In August 1985, four years after climbing Mt. Hood, he bagged number fifty, Gannett Peak, the only mountain he'd failed to summit on his first try. "There are still only about 100 people who have done all fifty," he says. "More people have climbed Mt. Everest."

In 1987 *Outside* magazine published his notice saying he'd like to hear from other highpointers. Thirty people replied. Before you could say "bulk postage," Jack's circle of like-minded mountain pen pals evolved into a nationwide club. By 1991 there were 350 members. Today the club has more than 2,300.

When we left "Jakk's Kottage," we followed Longacre over to Taum Sauk Mountain State Park. Bypassing the paved 1,080-foot wheelchair-accessible path that heads from the parking lot to the 1,772-foot summit, he led us through woods saturated from the torrential rain the day before to the polished granite summit marker. Bordered by red crusher stone, it was backed by a smooth boulder of rhyolite with deep cracks and splotches of lichen. To the left of the boulder a sturdy oak stood guard.

Had Nels and I visited this forest of twisted oak and hickory without Jack, we would have enjoyed a tranquil walk in the woods. But accompanied by the steward of Taum Sauk, the empty forest became animated. After tidying up the area like a mother hen, he showed us where the marker had been previously, before Paul Zumwalt, the author of *Fifty State Summits*, surveyed the area and had it moved to its current location.

Early on, Jack impressed me as something of a lovable kook. Even on a cold Friday in February, on a spot where he's stood more than sixty times in the past five years, Jack posed for a photo in a big ol' hillbilly hat. He unfurled an American flag, leaned back against the tree, and flashed a rakish grin. It was vintage Jack—simple, old-fashioned, fun.

But his hijinks are balanced by a pensive, sober streak, quite close to the surface. Longacre is a solitary, restless man who has found peace in the Ozarks as "the highest permanent resident in Missouri."

Before heading off, Jack told us that when he dies he wants some of his ashes to be sprinkled on each of the fifty highpoints. At a recent highpointers convention, he mentioned his plan to his eighty-nine-year-old friend Paul Zumwalt. A native of Illinois, Zumwalt thought it was a great idea and volunteered to place Longacre's ashes on Charles Mound. Longacre, who is twenty-five years younger, said, "Uh, Paul, I was kind of hoping to outlive you."

Nels and I cracked up, as did Jack. Another highpoint first: sharing a belly laugh about death with a man who's looking it in the eye. ▲

ARKANSAS

Magazine Mountain: *Somewhere between Havana and Hogeye*

A Southern Tour

**Highest Elevation
2,753 feet**

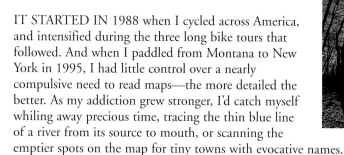

IT STARTED IN 1988 when I cycled across America, and intensified during the three long bike tours that followed. And when I paddled from Montana to New York in 1995, I had little control over a nearly compulsive need to read maps—the more detailed the better. As my addiction grew stronger, I'd catch myself whiling away precious time, tracing the thin blue line of a river from its source to mouth, or scanning the emptier spots on the map for tiny towns with evocative names.

Prior to this project, Arkansas was one of three states I'd never set foot in (Alaska and Louisiana were the others). In fact, until we left Taum Sauk in Missouri, I'd spent so little time looking at Arkansas on the map I could scarcely have told you it is bordered by Missouri, Tennessee, Oklahoma, and Texas. But as Nels drove the deserted back roads through hills dotted with naked, spiky-looking trees, I opened the atlas and made up for lost time.

Located between the Ozarks to the north and the Ouachitas to the south in western Arkansas, Magazine Mountain sits roughly halfway between Paris and Havana. Billed as "the gateway to Magazine Mountain," Paris is home to the state championship grape stomp as well as an international butterfly festival. Arkansas is blessed with more than the usual number of small towns with Old World names: Damascus, Jerusalem, Holland, and Scotland. On the map, these sit in stark contrast to down-home names like Waveland, Needmore, Romance, Blue Ball, Rose Bud, Nimrod, Hogeye, Greasy Corner, and Smackover. Not to mention Pocahontas, Biggers, and Oil Trough, which we drove through.

With its jagged diagonal border to the east (courtesy of the Mississippi River), Arkansas' profile looks like a page that's been torn abruptly from a book. Halfway between Fort Smith and Little Rock in the Arkansas River Valley are the highest peaks in the state—Nebo, Petit Jean, and Magazine—which one brochure said "rise like islands in the sky."

Magazine Mountain State Park protects 2,200 acres of the plateau-like summit. Though the highpoint is less than 3,000 feet, the ride through the park offered surprising vistas of river valleys, canyons, and distant mountains. We parked in the empty Cameron Bluff Campground and walked across the road to a narrow trail. Half a mile later, we stood on top in a clearing of ash and oak. Wet red clay stuck to our boots and splattered the bottoms of our pants. There were two wooden benches, a bunch of stumps, and a pile of rocks in a pit before a sturdy sign that read, "Signal Hill, Highest Point in Arkansas, 2,753 feet." Given the panoramic views we'd had en route, the non-view from the summit of Magazine Mountain was supremely anticlimactic.

"I'm a dead man," said Nels, a refrain I'd grown accustomed to.

We returned to the car and headed to Cameron Bluff Overlook, a two-minute drive away, on the north flank of Magazine Mountain. Striated 200-foot sandstone cliffs with huge melting icicles overlooked a valley filled with bare trees. As Nels set up his tripod, I walked around the bend to the next bluff 100 yards away to model. I moved cautiously along the edge, staring at wispy clouds streaked across the sky like watermarks on a beach. I stood in the wind longer than I cared to, feeling the pull of all that air below my feet. It was easy to see why this park was a playground for rock climbers and hang gliders.

When Nels was finished with me, I walked to the bend between the bluffs and headed down the steep embankment, clutching gnarled cedars and stunted

oaks. The fractured sandstone underneath a thick layer of dried leaves made the footing even more precarious. I stopped halfway down and looked up. The jagged wall was a petrified tapestry colored pink, red, gray, yellow, and white— as if a child had been allowed to decorate the world's largest layer cake.

The display I'd read at the Visitor Center earlier reframed the way I looked at this geological time capsule: 300 million years ago Magazine Mountain was covered by a swampy, tropical forest bordering a delta. Vast quantities of sand and mud were deposited in the shape of a giant fan. Fifty million years later (give or take a few million), shifting continental plates smashed into each other. This colossal collision turned western Arkansas into a mountainous mess. As the millenniums rolled by, these buckled layers of compressed sandstone and shale were eroded by weather, wind, and ancient rivers long since gone. Though I'm more interested in geography than geology, equipped with just that much information, I saw the layers of stone as rings on a giant sequoia; only these spanned the passage of time from the Paleozoic era to the second Bush Administration.

By 3:00, the greasy bacon and cheese omelet I'd eaten at Cathy's Kitchen near Subiaco had long since come unglued from my ribs, and I was hungry again. We climbed back in the car and drove south on Route 309 through Havana to Hot Springs, the boyhood home of Bill Clinton; an hour or two later, we passed the exit for Hope, his humble birthplace. I checked the map to see how far we were from Louisiana. There on Route 65 I spotted the town of Clinton, within spitting distance of Crabtree, Bee Branch, and Choctaw. ▲

LOUISIANA   Driskill Mountain: *A Final Resting Spot*

A Southern Tour

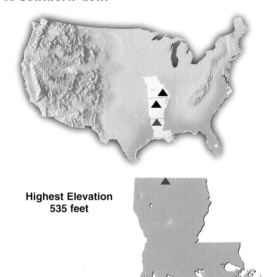

**Highest Elevation
535 feet**

WE ARRIVED AT EIGHT in the morning expecting to see parishioners in their Sunday best gathered in front of the Mt. Zion Presbyterian Church. Even though we'd only read that the church existed, we hoped to hear the congregation belting out hymns, or at least to meet one of the descendants of James Christopher Driskill, the Georgia farmer who arrived in these parts in the 1830s and bought 300-plus acres, including the 535-foot highpoint that bears his name.

Instead, we turned off a quiet two-lane country road into an empty parking lot where the loudest noise was our car tires crunching crushed stone. The Mt. Zion Presbyterian Church, a one-room, red-brick building, sat in front of the Driskill Memorial Cemetery. Two outhouses (his and hers?) stood near the woods to the left of the church; a picnic pavilion was on the right. While the

small, fenced-in cemetery was well maintained, the church's broken, boarded-up basement windows said that many a Sunday had passed since anyone had praised the Lord in this modest structure in northern Louisiana.

Despite the deserted feel, despite that it was an overcast, chilly Sunday in January—Super Bowl Sunday to be precise—despite that we were about to head up the third-lowest highpoint in the country, we were intrigued. The vacant church and humble cemetery filled with dozens of Driskills gave the highpoint a very personal feel.

We started out on the west side of the church, sidestepping rust-colored puddles on a flat trail with deep tire tracks that took us past a red radio tower. There were two forks in the mile-long trail and more than a few "No Trespassing" signs punctuated with bullet holes. (Deer hunting season had ended last month, but I was glad I was in a bright orange rain jacket.) We headed down the wrong spur and turned around at a rusted gate secured with a thick chain, then headed up a gentle slope covered with oak leaves and pine needles. Clumps of glistening moss decorated the steeply banked sides of the eroded trail. Tree roots poking through the red soil groped for nourishment.

Twenty minutes after starting out, we stood in a clearing in the woods next to a waist-high cairn of rocks flecked with moss and lichen. A pair of wire-framed glasses sat atop the cairn as if it were a night table. The bespectacled stone appeared to be a face surveying the scene. To a seriously near-sighted highpointer like me, these prescription glasses raised some important questions: Who owned them? How long had they been here? How had the visually impaired hiker navigated the winding trail back to the parking lot? Admittedly these aren't questions typically contemplated on a mountaintop, but they were unavoidable on the highest point of Louisiana.

It was windless and quiet up top, except for a few chatty birds and the occasional muted whoosh of car tires on the wet road below. There was no view from where we stood. As Nels focused on the glasses (this after a lengthy photo shoot of the outhouses), I perused the logbook housed in an ammo box near the cairn. A teenaged couple who had signed in as "Duffy and Dilfy" wrote that this was a "great place to have sex." Another duo had celebrated their thirty-ninth wedding anniversary with a peaceful walk in the woods. And a playful sort from Ruston wrote, "I am buried beneath the rock pile. Can someone call my Mom and tell her I'll be late for dinner?"

We returned to the cemetery. I'm not exactly sure why, but I've always enjoyed strolling through cemeteries. Perhaps it's because they're typically quiet and elegant—a combination of golf course and temple—and offer clues about strangers in the sparse details etched in stone. James Christopher "Grancer" Driskill (1817-1901) had had eight sons and one daughter and all but two had stayed in the area. I couldn't find the old man's plot, but as I walked from stone to stone on the pliant red soil, I counted about thirty of his kin buried here. Some of the names—Harlton Guyon Driskill, for example—were as southern as fried green tomatoes. Many had been soldiers. The weathered stone of Otis Driskill said that he had been killed on Okinawa on April 24, 1945. He was 29. One Sally Anderson Driskill (born in 1844) buried four of her eight children before she came to her final resting place here in 1910.

By 3:00 we began driving north toward Mississippi. We hadn't seen a soul all day. Nothing eventful had happened. But the hours we'd spent on the Driskill's spread had been moving. A dozen miles down the road was a monument where the murderous, thieving duo of Bonnie and Clyde had been ambushed by lawmen on May 23, 1934. We considered visiting the site, but after more than an hour of walking among the dead, we decided to push on. Besides, 300 miles down the road in New Orleans, raucous football fans were lubricating their vocal chords prior to Super Bowl XXXVI, which was set to kick off later in the day. Studying the map, I had high hopes that we'd be able to make it to Oxford, find a hotel, order a pizza, and settle in front of the tube before the end of the first half. ▲

MISSISSIPPI

Woodall Mountain: *Fire on the Mountain*

A Southern Tour

**Highest Elevation
806 feet**

WOODALL MOUNTAIN is known as America's bloodiest highpoint. During the Civil War, roughly 300,000 Union and Confederate troops fought more than 100 skirmishes within a twenty-mile radius of the 806-foot highpoint. And in the Battle of Iuka on September 19, 1862, Union cannon fire rained on Confederate troops from the top of what was then known as Yow Hill. The conflict waged around the mountain in the northeast corner of Mississippi was so fierce, a third of those who fought died.

The mountain's violent past has another notable chapter. In 1887 a fire destroyed Iuka's Tishomingo County Courthouse and all of its records, including evidence in a murder case. Zephaniah H. Woodall, the county sheriff, suspected arson. Soon after the fire, the densely wooded Yow Hill was renamed after the sheriff. I couldn't find any information about the trial or why Woodall was so honored, but it seemed as if the fourth-lowest highpoint in the country had witnessed more than its fair share of man's inhumanity to man.

In *Confederates in the Attic*, Tony Horowitz called the backwoods of Mississippi, "a myth-encrusted badlands for so many Americans." Having read William Faulkner, Eudora Welty, Barry Hannah, Tennessee Williams, and Larry Brown, I brought on this trip a kaleidoscope of vivid and violent images of Mississippi—some fact and some fiction—that I saw come to life during our drive north and east across the state. When we crossed the Mississippi River at Vicksburg, I remembered hearing Shelby Foote's mellifluous drawl discussing Grant's military campaign in which more than 30,000 rebel soldiers died. The fallow fields of cotton, countless Confederate flags, and elegant white homes with columns made me feel far from home, almost as if I were in another country. It was as Henry Miller wrote in *The Air-Conditioned Nightmare*, "The old South was plowed under. But the ashes are still warm."

The following morning we stopped at a grocery store/bait shop just south of Iuka. The owner was a chatty woman in her late fifties with dyed blond hair, plenty of make-up, and a belly that made the American flag on her sweatshirt billow at the bottom. It was 10 a.m. and she was flipping burgers for a handful of men in work pants and baseball caps, who were sipping coffee and smoking as they stared up at a TV broadcasting CNN. Half a dozen huge animal heads mounted in the back stared glassy-eyed past enough fishing equipment to scare most of the catfish out of Tishomingo County.

My hamburger-flipping friend told me that the local folks tended to hold on to their land. "The countryside hasn't changed all that much since I was a girl," she said. Her thirty-year-old son had recently purchased 185 acres of woods north of Booneville. "He'll die on that land," she said matter-of-factly.

I asked her if she'd ever been up Woodall Mountain.

"I've seen it all my life," she said, "but never bothered to find the turnoff to drive on up."

I asked if there were any monuments in town to the Battle of Iuka.

"Sure isn't," she said. She recommended we go to Corinth or Shiloh.

We drove up a steep, twisting gravel road to the summit. It was 40°F and windy on top. There were four radio towers and a concrete table and bench. The sign that had once proclaimed Woodall Mountain the highest point in Mississippi was missing, leaving a broken frame. The summit, our forty-fifth, looked as if it had seen more than a few redneck picnics. Empty bottles of booze, cigarette butts, plastic bags, wrappers, and spent fireworks littered the circular dirt clearing. Next to the USGS marker was a foot-high, red-plastic tube with a snarling cat on the side. It read, "Black Cat Artillery Shells, a total of thirty-six different effects." The brush and trees obstructed all but a narrow view of power lines running downhill. It was hardly a piece of real estate worth living on, let alone dying over.

Nels disappeared behind a radio transformer, muttering about the tragic photo ops; I sat at the cold concrete table and read about the events of September 19, 1862. Five days after Confederate General Sterling Price burned a Union supply depot in Iuka, Grant instructed General William Rosecrans to attack Price's troops from Woodall Mountain to the southeast. After the fighting began, the plan called for Union troops to swoop in from the west, driving the graycoats into the Tennessee River. It was a sound strategy, but the attack from the west never occurred.

Throughout the day, Union troops showered the Confederates with heavy artillery from Woodall Mountain and the surrounding high ground. Rebel forces, wedged in the dense woods in a nearby ravine, were able to storm the hill and commandeer half a dozen Union cannons, forcing a Union retreat. Of the more than 4,000 Union troops, 1,482 lay dead or wounded; the Confederates lost 700 out of 3,200 men. With no monument to mark the battle, I wondered how many of those who fired the ersatz artillery shells knew

that a bloody fight had been waged from this spot.

At the intersection of U.S. 72 and State Road 25, the center of the battlefield, we headed back through Corinth, once a pivotal rail junction that had been prized highly by both sides. (The east/west line still runs two miles north of Woodall Mountain.) In Tennessee we drove by the turnoff to Shiloh National Military Park where Confederate General Albert S. Johnson led a surprise attack that killed 24,000 of Grant's men. There are thousands who reenact these brutal battles each year and many more who still fly the Reb flag. As a Yankee interloper I can't pretend to understand the effect this has had on the Southern psyche. But back at home, I nodded in agreement when I read something by Willie Morris, who grew up in Yazoo City. He referred to his feelings for the South as "good ol' boy" love. Of his home state he wrote, "Mississippi has always been a bewitched and tragic ground, yet it's also a land of heroism and nobility; a land which has honored those of us of all races who possess the courage and the imagination of the resources given us on this haunted terrain. I love Mississippi, and I hope the best of it will endure." ▲

WEST VIRGINIA

Spruce Knob: *Montani Semper Liberi*

A Southern Tour

**Highest Elevation
4,861 feet**

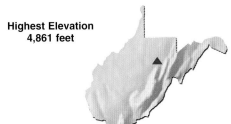

MY FRIEND CHRIS, a playwright who teaches squash in Manhattan, loves to say how much he hates just about everything. Cell phones, Los Angeles, and bagels with too much cream cheese are three of his pet peeves. A few years ago, he went to West Virginia for some outdoor recreation. When he returned, he couldn't stop raving about rock climbing at Seneca Rocks and riding his mountain bike along exposed ridges and down dried boulder-strewn stream beds. "The place is a gold mine!" he said. He was so positive, so uncynical—so un-Chris-like. After his second trip, he said he was thinking about buying a cabin in the Monongahela National Forest. Wow, I thought, the man is losing his edge.

With forty-five peaks down, this trip at the end of February was to be our final foray in the Lower 48 until we headed to Alaska in June. I picked up Nels in Baltimore on a cold, sunny afternoon and headed for the hills. Around Front Royal, Virginia, the alluring dark-green profile of the Blue Ridge Mountains appeared. We turned off Route 81 in Harrisonburg, the home of James Madison University, and headed west on Route 33 toward West Virginia. Before you could list the rest of the founding fathers, the squiggly red line on the map delivered us into the most spectacular mountain landscape I'd seen in the East—scenery that Thomas Jefferson said was "worth a voyage across the Atlantic." No wonder the state is often called "the Switzerland of America," and that Chris was so impressed.

Spruce Knob is located at the bottom of the eastern panhandle in the Monongahela National Forest just across the Virginia state line. Though it's less than twenty-five miles as the crow flies, getting there on terra firma isn't easy. We wiggled up and down the Appalachian and Shenandoah Mountains, past road signs riddled with bullet holes, decrepit trailers, and tiny churches perched by the side of the road. Our average speed was approximately 25 mph, and we were racing against nightfall. When I wasn't making sure we didn't plunge off the serpentine highway, I was gazing up at jagged fins of white-gray rock or into a grassy valley dotted with cattle and rocks.

At 5 p.m. we slowed as we passed through Judy Gap, a town too small for more than a few Judys, and headed west into the Spruce Knob–Seneca Rocks National Recreation Area. As we climbed higher, patches of snow on the hills became snowy fields, and finally even the dirt road was a rutted carpet of snow and ice. The mountains stretching toward the horizon to our left looked like a miniature version of the Rockies.

We parked in an empty lot on top, a short walk from the 4,861-foot summit, and stepped out of the car into a frigid wind. We hurried into our cold-weather gear like firemen answering a call, and hustled to the forty-foot lookout tower along a snowy walkway. On the top deck, the full wrath of the wind hit like a breaking wave. My eyes were tearing; my fingers and toes grew numb. The mountains dissolved beautifully into the night, but all I could think about was that I was freezing my ass off.

On the way up, Nels and I had talked about throwing sleeping bags under the tower so that we wouldn't have to leave and drive back in the morning, but that idea was quickly squashed. Sleep out in anything less than a –40°F bag and you'd end up as stiff as a steak in a meat locker.

Nels gave me the thumbs up and I hustled back.

"It's freezing!" I shouted

"Freezing!" he replied.

That pretty much covered it.

By 6:50 p.m., we were back in the car with the heater on high, headed down the mountain. In Franklin (population 914) we dropped $38 at the Thompson Motel, which, praise be, had its own restaurant. Our waitress told us that she'd grown up on the mountain road we'd taken to Spruce Knob. "I drove ten miles down the mountain to go to school in the morning," she said, with a distinctive drawl, "and ten miles back up in the afternoon." Times were tough around here, she said, especially after the lone factory in town closed a few years ago. Some folks raised cattle and sheep, but when I asked her how most people made a living in Franklin, she shrugged her shoulders.

Later, I read that West Virginia has always been one of the poorest states in the country. Before the Civil War, West Virginia and Virginia were one state. The Virginians, blessed with fertile farmlands, relied heavily on slave labor, while West Virginians scratched out a living in the hills raising livestock. Slaves were taxed at a lower rate than farm animals, which was a source of contention between the two sides of the state. The ideological division between the two regions became as well-defined as the mountains that separated them, and in 1861 West Virginia seceded to become a separate state. While the rugged terrain has imposed stiff economic and social challenges on its residents, the state motto remains, *Montani Semper Liberi*—Mountaineers are always free.

We returned to Spruce Knob in the morning. The sun was bright, but the wind remained fierce and the cold nearly as intense. Features that had been dulled by the dwindling light were now sharply defined. The flat gray stones in a field bordered by snow appeared artfully arranged; one-sided red spruce, covered in rime ice and deformed by the prevailing westerly wind, ringed the summit like a broken fence. A manicured glade just below the summit, dotted with a dozen huge, gray boulders (a Stonehenge in the making?) seemed out of place with the rest of the shaggy terrain. Everywhere you looked there were snowy mountains with steep ridges in shades of green.

Walking around the summit on the Whispering Pines Trail, I thought of the e-mail Chris sent me when I told him where I was going. "I loved Spruce Knob," he wrote. "I remember the rocks were sharp and jagged. That's important because I think it represents the appeal of West Virginia. Every ride or hike I've been on there has been rough and diverse. West Virginia is always gnawing at you. It's a constant, if not epic, challenge."

Take me home, country roads. The cynic from New York had clearly left home without it—cynicism, that is. ▲

NORTH CAROLINA — Mt. Mitchell: *The Good Doctor*

**Highest Elevation
6,684 feet**

YEARS AGO I RODE A BICYCLE the length of the 469-mile Blue Ridge Parkway en route from Florida to New York City. Approximately thirty miles outside of Asheville, North Carolina, a hip town at the base of the Blue Ridge, I passed the turnoff for Mt. Mitchell. I considered riding up the twisting two-lane road, but I'd been climbing nearly continuously all morning and decided to push on. "I'll come back some other time," I thought.

In March 2001, Nels and I sat in Asheville staring despondently at the heavy snow that had closed the Blue Ridge Parkway. One year later, we were back. While the conditions were a lot better, they still stunk. On a nice day, Mt. Mitchell is a scenic drive with a short stroll to the top. But when we turned off the Blue Ridge on to Route 128, the driving rain was starting to freeze and the road was a slick, slushy mess.

The pinnacle of the mile-high Black Mountains stands 6,684 feet—the highest point east of the Mississippi. According to the park's web site, the top of Mt. Mitchell is covered in clouds and fog eight out of ten days. ("Forested and forever misty," said one brochure.) The average annual snowfall is over eight feet, and it can snow any month of the year. The record low is −34°F. And on the western face, the wind commonly exceeds 100 mph. In other words, this harsh alpine environment is more like Canada than North Carolina.

Just after the turnoff, we approached a tunnel with icicles as big as an elephant's tusk dangling from the entrance.

"Looks like the gates to hell," Nels said, "only colder."

"At least there won't be too much traffic," I said.

It took us nearly two hours to reach the deserted parking lot on top. As we sat in the car, listening to the wind and freezing rain batter the car, and trying to work up the courage to get out, a snowplow drove by, stopped, and backed up. A stout woman with a rumpled park service cap eyed us as if she thought we were casing the joint. She peered into our car and asked to see my driver's license. Clearly our presence on such a dog-shit day didn't compute. "We're about to close the road," she said.

The thought that we might be turned back from this mountain yet again galvanized us. We explained our mission, swore we wouldn't stay long, donned our storm gear and scurried off across a sheet of ice.

The trail to the lookout tower was all of 285 yards away, but with the wind and freezing rain my eyeglasses fogged up; creeping up the icy path, I felt like a near-sighted man on a balance beam. Were it clear, we'd have seen mountains rising from the Cane and Toe River valleys to ridges covered with spruce and fir—the dark-green, nearly black trees that gave the range its name. We'd have admired the nearby peaks of Grandfather, Roan, Tablerock, and Hawksbill, as well as the Craggy, Blue Ridge, and Smoky Mountains, seventy-five miles away.

Instead, as Nels tried to photograph this inhospitable place, I jogged in place inside the snowy tower listening to the 50 mph wind crash around me. When he came in seeking refuge from a particularly nasty squall, Nels said, "It's like shooting in a frozen car wash."

I wandered outside to the pointy black fence around the grave of Dr. Eliasha Mitchell (1793-1857). In 1835 Dr. Mitchell, a clergyman and science professor at the University of North Carolina, set out to prove that the Black Mountains were the highest peaks east of the Mississippi. Relying on local guides, he doggedly hiked up and down the rugged mountains—forty miles in two or three days—trying to figure out which of the nine 6,000-foot peaks was the tallest in the range. There were no trails, and he had no maps. It's amazing he survived that trip, let alone two additional trips he made in 1838 and 1844.

Mitchell measured the mountains using barometric pressure readings. Initially, he believed that the tallest mountain in the Blacks (which he named after himself) was 6,476 feet. When he returned for the third time in 1844, he said that Mt. Gibbs—not Mitchell—stood 6,672 feet, making it the highest. (He was 12 feet off.) In a roundabout way, his error proved to be fatal.

Eleven years later, Senator Thomas Clingman, a former student of Mitchell's, measured both mountains, pronounced Mitchell the tallest, and took credit for being the first to accurately measure the loftiest peak in the East. Determined to defend his claim, the sixty-two-year-old doctor returned to the mountain in 1857. Walking at nightfall alone down a creek bed, he slipped, fell twenty feet and drowned in a pool below a waterfall. A year after he was buried in Asheville, Eliasha Mitchell was laid to rest at the top of the mountain. Never had I visited a more fitting burial ground.

I'd been running in place inside the lookout tower for half an hour when Nels said he was finished. We were driving down the road just as our ever-vigilant ranger drove up, intending to usher us out. We both stopped. I thanked her for her patience. She stared down from her truck and nodded. Her mood hadn't seemed to improve any. I suppose that when the mountain you patrol is named after a doctor who died on its slopes, you just can't be too careful. ▲

VIRGINIA Mt. Rogers: *Don't Handle the Ponies*

A Southern Tour

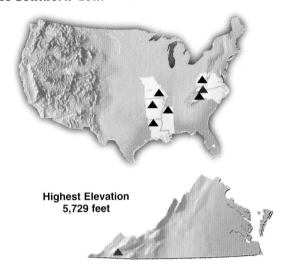

**Highest Elevation
5,729 feet**

IF ATTITUDE IS EVERYTHING, as my mother liked to say, then Nels and I had a lot of work in front of us. After a solid week of hideous weather down South, we pulled into the nearly deserted parking lot in Mount Rogers National Recreation Area, 154,000 protected acres located in the southwest tip of the state named after Virginia, the Queen of England. Rain fell steadily. The sound of trees swaying in the wind was audible even with the windows closed tightly.

We stared out into the fog at a fallow field with all the enthusiasm of Enron executives facing a Congressional hearing. Mt. Rogers was supposed to be our forty-ninth summit; the last highpoint in our southern swing prior to our grand finale in Alaska in June. Driven by our respective time constraints, a patient but prodding editor, and an overwhelming desire to complete a project that seemed never-ending, we'd pushed hard on this road trip, not budgeting extra time for obstacles like road closings—which turned us away in Tennessee. Since we'd been stymied on Clingmans Dome, the combination of crappy

weather, the thought of having to return for just one peak, and a textbook case of road-weariness left us on the wrong side of glum.

Once we geared up and walked into the woods, nature worked its magic. The brisk air and dark, jagged rocks covered with lizard-green moss transported us to a far more mysterious and exotic landscape than either of us had expected. Close your eyes and you feel as if you're in the Scottish Highlands. The patter of raindrops falling through the dense forest provided perfect acoustics and ample protection from the fierce wind. It was downright cozy in our soggy enclave.

Forty minutes down the trail, we realized that we were lost. Nels, our pigheaded navigator, had led us in the opposite direction on the wrong trail. I tried to remain serene—and outwardly I suppose I succeeded—but when we returned to the parking lot to start over, my mood, which had been shaky to begin with, stunk. It was in the sewer system. Like I said, attitude is everything.

Feeling guilty that he'd led us astray, Nels resorted to an old standby: humor. Not far from the parking lot—the trail had been virtually in front of where we parked—we passed a sign that read: "Don't handle or molest the ponies!"

"Isn't that sign redundant?" Nels asked earnestly. Though I rarely pass up an opportunity to demonstrate my immaturity, at the moment I wasn't eager to discuss the sexual politics of ponies. This time, I let silence do my talking.

Nels wasn't done. "Why even put the idea in people's minds? Now it's all I can think about."

I made a mental note to have a chat with Nels' girlfriend, the daughter of a pastor and soybean farmer from southern Illinois, for Pete's sake.

Headed up the muddy Rhododendron Trail through a meadow littered with pony poop and granite boulders, I eased into my rugged surroundings. Once again Nels and I were walking purposely up a trail, bantering as we'd done forty-seven times before. So we were one mountain "behind" where we'd wanted to be, so we were walking in heavy mist and gusts of wind on a dank Sunday in early March. We were, as Nels had often pointed out, out making a living doing something we loved. One thing I've always noted about my photographer friend is how stinkingly good-humored he is. Give the man a goal, a camera, and a package of Twizzlers and nothing gets him down.

Half a mile higher on the 5,729-foot mountain (named after Dr. William Barton Rogers, Virginia's first state geologist and the founder of the Massachusetts Institute of Technology), we turned west on the white-blazed Appalachian Trail to Rhododendron Gap. Had we been here, say, on a clear day in June, we'd have enjoyed hundreds of rhododendron painting the mountainside purple. (If you can't make it to the mountain in the summer, pick up the Marion phonebook; the riotous scene is on the cover.)

But walking in fog and wind that bit harder as we headed higher, the summit was our sole goal. By the time we were a mile high, the stunted vegetation was covered in ice. With the windchill it was well below zero. At the Thomas Knob Shelter, a crude, three-sided log structure half a mile from the summit, I jogged in place to restore feeling to my toes. I'd not brought my Gore-Tex gloves and my wool pair had gotten wet while we'd wandered on the wrong trail hours ago. Suddenly hypothermia felt like a real risk. Only later did I learn that the boreal forest on Mt. Rogers is the same type found in Nova Scotia, 800 miles north.

We stumbled about looking for the true summit. It was nearly 4:30 p.m. and the cold seemed nearly suffocating. Finally, we found the metal marker. Surrounded by fir trees, there was no view, so we hustled down back into the teeth of the wind. The cold was startling. If I lost fingers or toes on the highpoint of Virginia I'd be a laughingstock back home.

Halfway down the mountain, we passed three wild ponies grazing behind a cluster of stunted trees. Nels held his index finger to his lips. He was eager to get a photograph. Bent at the waist—don't ask me why, it seemed more clandestine—we crept closer, keen on a Kodak moment. Twice, behind a rock, we communicated with hand signals like soldiers waiting in ambush. We were less than fifty feet away when Nels whispered, "The brown one with the thick mane is lovely!"

Given the cold, encroaching darkness, and our cautious approach, the comment caught me by surprise. I began laughing like a hyena. Nels fell to pieces and the ponies vanished into the mist.

Back in the car, I cranked up the heater and stomped my frozen feet. Even now, if Nels just says the word "pony" I start to smirk. In retrospect, the lesson I learned had less to do with attitude—I'd known that a positive mindset is crucial long ago—but I'd failed to realize how crucial timing is on a cold mountain. ▲

TENNESSEE
Clingmans Dome: *The Place of Blue Smoke*

A Southern Tour

**Highest Elevation
6,643 feet**

APPROACHING KNOXVILLE, I gazed out the window of our rental car at an endless sea of mountains bordered by the Tennessee River, which twisted into the horizon like a gnarly limb. We were on our way to 6,643-foot Clingmans Dome, but with Denali just over a week away it was hard to stay focused on the mountain at hand. I had spent most of my early morning flight reading *Below Another Sky*, Rick Ridgeway's account of returning to a mountain in China with the daughter of the friend who'd climbed it with him. Ridgeway and his friend had been swept down the mountain by an avalanche and the friend had died. With the biggest physical challenge of this project just ahead, I contemplated the role that risk and adventure have played in my life.

We'd been turned back from the mountain three months earlier on a stormy day when we discovered the road to the summit was still closed for the winter. We could have hiked the seven miles to the summit, but, well, we didn't. Now it was June and the sun was shining. Six miles outside of the Great Smoky Mountains National Park, we hit a wall of traffic in the tourist town of Pigeon Forge. Had we more time, say two years, we might have stopped at

Splash World, Dolly Parton's twenty-five-acre water park. In Gatlinburg, the town that borders the national park, we were sorely tempted by the eighteen-hole "Hillbilly" miniature golf course, but we had a job to do and steadfastly pressed on.

It was an odd juxtaposition, these two towns and the 520,976-acre park with 800 miles of trails. The rugged landscape features 1,600 species of flowering plants, 120 species of native trees, 200 species of birds, plenty of black bears and, with thirty species, it's the salamander capital of America. Though approximately ten million visitors come each year—more than to any other national park—a ranger told us that the trails are rarely crowded.

Just inside the park, we stopped to pick up a bearded, white-haired hitchhiker who stood with a walking stick and backpack at his feet. His name was Bill Alexander and after an all-day hike he was eleven miles from his truck.

A retired environmental scientist from Knoxville with a mellifluous Tennessee accent, he called himself a "mountain poet, artisan, and basket maker." His "fifth granddad" was a Scots-Irishman named Oliver Alexander who came to Tennessee during the Revolutionary War. Bill had started hiking a few years before he and his wife split. Though they're together again, he keeps returning to fulfill his goal of hiking every mile of every trail in the park.

When we dropped Bill at his truck, he reached inside and handed us a thin booklet of his poems, which he autographed. As I flipped through it, he closed his eyes and began reciting a few of his favorites. As far as poetry appreciation goes, I tend to favor ribald limericks, but Bill's delivery was so heartfelt it was a pleasure to listen to his simple rhyming words. "Trails are rocks and roots and dirt," he began. "Yet, they have souls, gathered from all those who passed, step by step, so bold. Stop, and listen for the quiet, and you will see and hear, all those who passed before, like looking through a mirror."

Bill pointed out that we were standing across the road from the Appalachian Trail. "Clingmans Dome is the highest point on the entire trail," he said. Nels and I had planned on walking the half-mile paved path to the top. Instead, we shouldered our packs and headed toward highpoint forty-nine, 3.6 miles up the Appalachian Trail. Poetry will do that to you.

Two hours later we stood at the foot of what has to be the funkiest observation tower on any of the fifty highpoints. Standing fifty-four-feet tall atop the mountain named after Thomas Lanier Clingman—a lawyer, entrepreneur, Civil War general, inventor, scientist, explorer, and Senator who died a penniless eccentric in 1897—the structure has a central pillar that looks like a cross between a flying saucer and an air traffic control tower. A wheelchair-accessible ramp curves gracefully over the spindly pines to the top of the tower, somewhat like a bobsled run. Nels said, "This could be the seventeenth hole at the Hillbilly mini-golf course." Half-way up the ramp, a teenager quipped, "Beam me up, Scotty."

No matter what you thought of the tower, there was nothing goofy about the view, a vista of dark, rounded mountains in a bluish-gray haze that extended as far as the eye could see. The Cherokee called this land the "Place of the Blue Smoke." Later I read that the average viewing distance on top of old Smoky is twenty-two miles; on a clear day you can see for 100 miles into seven states. This day, I estimated visibility at about thirty-seven miles.

We hung out for two hours amidst a steady stream of visitors. Most arrived breathlessly; many complained how tough the half-mile ascent had been—and virtually everyone said "Wow!" the moment they confronted the 360-degree view.

Fitness level aside, we came for the same reason. When I got back home, I found a poem in the mountain philosopher's little book that pretty much summed it up: "So while traveling in this life, enjoy the mountains and sand. For our time here passes, like frost from the land." ▲

NUMBER FIFTY

- Alaska

ALASKA Denali: *The Great One*

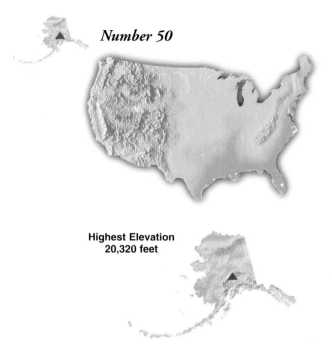

**Highest Elevation
20,320 feet**

WE WERE SIX CLIMBERS and two guides from Alpine Ascents International, treading our way slowly up the steep, snowy slopes of the highest peak in North America. After two rest days in the thin air at Camp IV, we carried food and supplies through deep snow up a long slope that deposited us on a modest-sized ledge at 15,400 feet. We rounded a corner, clipped onto the fixed line and started up the headwall, 800 vertical feet of snow and ice at a 45- to 60-degree slope—the steepest climbing on the entire route. An hour and a half of respiratory angst later, we stood on a ridge at 16,200 feet in a 30-mph wind staring at the exposed, rocky ridge that disappeared over the horizon like an evil serpent. We cached our supplies and returned to camp, drained and daunted by what lay ahead.

The next morning, Vern Tejas, our head guide, asked each of us how we felt. In fact, after two weeks on the mountain, the spryest among us felt like

elderly fish swimming upstream. Mike, a forty-nine-year-old stockbroker from Seattle, was battling a respiratory infection. He said he would try to make it to high camp, but he interrupted himself with a ferocious coughing fit and wasn't terribly convincing. Gary, at fifty-seven the oldest member of our group, was laboring but figured if we went slow enough he'd make it. Nels, who was physically strong but anxious about continuing, voted for a rest day.

But the weather was good and a few hours later we headed up. Forty-five minutes out of Camp IV, Mike sat on his pack, his head bowed, snot dripping from his sunburned nose. Co-guide John Colver, a thirty-six-year-old former British paratrooper, hustled up the hill and told Vern that Mike was done. At that point Gary, a tough Texan who'd done a tour in Vietnam and spent plenty of time in the cold, snowy mountains of Chile and Antarctica, said he didn't have the chops to continue either. Then Nels volunteered to join our

the name of twenty-one-year-old Chris Hooyman, one of the guides on our Mt. Rainier climb, a vibrant and skilled mountaineer. He had unclipped from the rope at 17,000 feet to help a fallen climber, slipped, failed to self-arrest and slid to his death. As Greg Childs wrote in the preface to Jonathan Waterman's *In The Shadow of Denali,* "As long as Denali stands, climbers will come, and some of them will die. It is an icon of American climbing, as identifiable as the Eiger Nordwand or Mount Everest."

We arrived on the mountain on June 12, after waiting all day for the weather to clear for our flight to the glacier. We crammed into the four-seater with plastic sleds, a twenty-one-day supply of food and enough Gore-Tex to stock a mountain-eering store, taxied down the runway and quickly left civilization behind. A sea of pines framed three rivers that flowed swiftly from the glacier. Jagged mountains of brown dirt and rock yielded to snowy peaks. We gazed out the window at a vast and violent glaciated landscape, flashing a thumb's-up or shouting "Awesome!"

We landed roughly at 7,200 feet on the Kahiltna Glacier. Two dozen brightly colored tents dotted the vast, crevassed slope like beach towels on the dunes of the Sahara. Mt. Hunter, a 14,573-foot monster, loomed over base camp, avalanches roaring down its slopes about every fourteen minutes. Mt. Foraker, a 17,400-foot giant across the way, sported a menacing lenticular cloud big enough to blot out downtown Anchorage. (A week later, three brothers died on Foraker.) As I stood in the thin air gawking at the amphitheater of mountains, Vern came over. "You know, I've seen climbers step out of the plane, take one look, and get on the next plane back to Talkeetna," he said.

If Denali is the greatest mountain in North America, then Tejas, who has climbed it nearly every year since 1978, is the greatest guide. His thirty-some ascents are probably an all-time high; however, he refuses to divulge the exact number for fear of sparking a record-setting chase with two other Alaskan guides. While Tejas is best known in climbing circles for pulling off the first solo winter ascent of Denali in 1988, his epic rescue of a stranded Korean climber on the Cassin Ridge has become an Alaskan legend. He's climbed Everest twice, parasailed off several of the seven summits, and seen more remote Alaskan wilderness than a peripatetic grizzly bear.

retreating comrades, following, he said, his gut instinct. We hugged and trudged in opposite directions. In a matter of minutes our collegial group of eight had become a gang of four.

When Harvard photographer and cartographer Bradford Washburn first climbed the 20,320-foot mountain via the West Buttress in 1951, he called it a "safe, steep, chilly scramble." After spending time in this immense glaciated landscape, I readily agreed with "steep" and "chilly." But safe? Perhaps to the intrepid Washburn, who had twice reached the top via the more treacherous Muldrow route in 1942 and '47 (the latter climb with his wife Barbara, the first woman to summit).

I'd read too many stories about vicious winds picking up a tent with its inhabitants, climbers disappearing into bottomless crevasses, and Arctic cold turning fingers and toes into black, lifeless stumps, to feel anything like safe. In Talkeetna, the tiny town where we caught an air taxi to the Kahiltna Glacier, Nels and I saw a memorial to climbers who've died on the mountain, We found

With his shaved head, dark eyebrows, black beret and the purple-and-red reversible climbing suit he designed himself, he is one of the most recognizable figures on North America's biggest hill. An accomplished musician, he typically climbs with a fiddle and harmonica. On our climb he carried a custom-built Martin guitar and played for hours each day. (His lone CD is called *Strummit from the Summit*.)

After our group split up around 15,000 feet, four of us went on to Camp V. Along with Vern and me was Dolly, a thirty-four-year-old Yale-educated lawyer who worked for Nike in Portland, and Rob, a laid-back attorney from Phoenix. We spent two oxygen-depleted days dug in behind five-foot walls of snow at 17,200 feet, resting for the summit push. While the views were breathtaking, simple tasks like eating, eliminating, and staying warm felt like federal projects. (Dehydrated sweet and sour pork gets old at any altitude but when you already have high-camp diarrhea, it's particularly grim.) When we woke on our third day, the wind above was ferocious, so we continued our lethargic waiting game. Dolly's cough worsened; Rob spent more time on his back than a streetwalker during Mardi Gras. I lost both my appetite and my desire to schmooze—clear signs that all was not right with the universe. We prayed for good weather so we could tag the top and get the hell out.

On Friday, June 28, Vern woke us at 7 a.m. "Show time, kids," he sang in a piercing, wake-the-dead voice—one part borscht-belt comedian, one part southern drill sergeant. The sky was clear, the wind manageable. It was our fifteenth day on the mountain. We nervously downed hot drinks and cold cereal, stuffed chemical warmers in our gloves and boots, donned stripped-down packs and headed breathlessly out of camp.

Vern walked the point, Dolly was second, I was third on the rope, and Rob batted clean-up. Vern had warned us that summit day would be our longest and hardest. "It's likely to be," he said at the start of the climb, "the hardest thing you do in your life." He was right. The first, and perhaps most dangerous, section on the route was an hour-and-a-half traverse of a 30-degree slope with a kicked-in trail that was about as wide as a shoebox. (The next day a solo climber fell to his death there.)

At 18,200 feet, we rested on a flat spot known as Denali Pass, added a few layers of clothing and continued along the ridgeline on the southwest face. During each break, Rob, who'd been strong for the past two weeks, sat lifelessly, not eating or drinking until Vern got on his case. Dolly said little but seemed solid. Just four hours into it, I silently wondered if I had the energy to get to the top.

Hours later, we stowed our packs at a plateau at 19,500 feet called the Football Field. The summit ridge seemed tantalizingly close. Vern said, "This is where lots of teams turn around."

We started toward a slope known appropriately as Pig Hill. Rob, who'd been virtually silent all day, managed to crack a joke, "It's ridiculously steep, but at least I'm exhausted!"

We trudged up, up, up, each in our own bubble of fatigue, but buoyed by Vern's strength. At the top of the endless hill we stared in disbelief at the sheer ridge that separated us from the summit. It was only 300 yards—100 vertical feet—but it was narrow, heart-attack narrow, and jagged, dropping off to oblivion on either side. I thought, "There's no bleepin' way I'm walking on that."

But when Vern said, "Giddy-up," I got up. For nearly forty minutes I kicked and re-kicked each breathless step with the concentration of a surgeon on the job. I don't mind admitting that I negotiated the worst ten feet on all fours.

And then we had the top to ourselves.

It was 5 p.m., sunny and clear. You could see for more than a hundred miles in all directions. The dirty tongue of the Ruth Glacier curved a path through a galaxy of snowy mountains. We hugged awkwardly in our heavy down coats and took a bunch of photos. It felt odd to be at the top without Nels, but I was too tired and happy—and too preoccupied with the descent— to dwell on my missing comrade. Vern, who'd carried the Martin guitar to the top, belted out a ballad he'd written. "Life is an adventure," he crooned. "Gonna keep explorin'/Don't wanna be no spectator, for it's far too borin'/Life's too precious, gonna keep explorin'." We lingered in the thin −15°F air for thirty minutes and then started anxiously down the ridge.

At 10 p.m. we were back at high camp. The sun was still high in the sky—it never sets in June—but it felt as if whole days had gone by. We downed mugs of hot chocolate and crawled into our sleeping bags as quickly as we could. I was too tired to celebrate, but I knew this day would stay with me for the rest of my life. Denali was the real reason I'd signed on to the book project five years ago. I'd wanted to climb the mountain for twenty years, ever since a college mate I admired sent me a copy of the diary he kept during his successful climb. He was a true adventurer; I was a wannabe. Now I had stood where he had stood, and it felt like a milestone.

The next morning we started down. The descent took us two days, and we only slept three hours. The four of us had to pick up and carry some of the equipment left behind by the other four, and our packs felt as if they were filled with lead. When we arrived at base camp, now empty save for the woman who coordinated the flights out, I was a sunburned, dehydrated, exhausted shell of a man. Even Vern finally seemed spent.

Thirty minutes before our plane was supposed to arrive, heavy, wet snow began to fall. "We could be here for a while," Vern said. "Let's set up camp." After days of dreaming of a hot shower and a real meal, the thought of spending another night on the mountain was grim. But two hours later, the snow stopped. We strapped on our snowshoes and, walking three abreast, stomped down the landing strip to give the pilot a smoother surface.

Then the sweetest sound I'd heard in eighteen days greeted us—the drone of a small prop plane. We welcomed our pilot from K2 Aviation as if he were Santa Claus.

And then we were in the air. In minutes, mountains wrapped in white turned brown. Colors we'd not seen for weeks—pine trees, birds, silty rivers—shouted to us. Just outside of Talkeetna, we flew under an immense double rainbow that spanned the horizon. It seemed too perfect to be real.

Thirty minutes later we were on terra firma in Talkeetna, experiencing a severe case of sensory overload Denali-style. We cleaned up and made our way to Cafe Michele, the finest in dining Talkeetna had to offer. We toasted each other, the mountain, Vern's leadership, Michele, the waitress, even the dog that lay in the parking lot.

Later, sorting my gear, back at the Alpine Ascents compound, I thought of a rank, ravaged-looking climber who'd landed in Talkeetna moments before we took off. As we passed each other on the airstrip I asked if he'd made it to the top. "Yeah, and it was freakin' hell!" he shouted. "But it's worth it; it's worth it!" Then he laughed maniacally.

Clearly the man needed to spend some time at sea level, but even in his oxygen-deprived state he'd nicely summed up the basic conundrum of climbing. I'd spent a lot of time on the mountain musing over Nels' decision to turn back at 16,200 feet. "I don't need the summit," he'd told me several times during the climb. That was a reasonable, even life-affirming, stance—after all, during our climb one man died on Denali and three died on neighboring Mt. Foraker. We had greatly reduced our risk by going with experienced guides, but not to zero.

The challenge I had set for myself was not to summit at all costs, but to go as far as the mountain and my strength would let me; to continue past the edge of my comfort zone to see what was on the other side. Nels and I have talked about this often since returning, and the conversation continues. What's clear is that the climb exceeded both of our expectations. More than any other mountain, Denali affected us in ways we're still deciphering. ▲

AFTERWORD

IN THE ANNALS of mountaineering, standing on top of all fifty state highpoints ranks right up there with, say, crossing America on a unicycle. It's ambitious, physically and logistically difficult, and more than a bit off the wall.

If you're not obsessed when you begin such a project, you probably will be after you've driven 5,000 miles, climbed two dozen highpoints, and realized that you're nearly halfway through. Leslie Stephen, a literary critic, historian, and mountaineer, could have delivered the keynote speech at a highpointers convention when he said: "I am a fanatic. I believe that the ascent of mountains forms an essential chapter in the complete duty of a man, and that it is wrong to leave any district without setting foot on its highest peak."

When Nels and I started the project, climbing all fifty was not so much a point of honor as a fun and funky way to indulge our adventure travel addiction. "We'll hammer it out in six months," he told me, beer in hand, from the comfort of his living room. That was in 1997. Five years later, we climbed Denali, highpoint number fifty.

Our first trip out West fit the bill. Though we didn't know all that much about mountaineering—okay, next to nothing—it was exciting to muck our way up these beautiful spots. Along the way, we passed through intriguing little towns and saw plenty of stunning country. We also listened to great music and laughed our car-weary backsides off.

The nervous energy I felt as we approached a mountain—via car and on foot—reminded me of driving to a rival's gymnasium when I played high school basketball. Rugged peaks like Boundary in Nevada, Kings in Utah, Borah in Idaho—mountains that I'd not heard of and would otherwise have never climbed—were a physical challenge and geographical treasure hunt with a vertical twist. No matter how lousy I felt on the way up or down, afterward I felt nourished.

Erik Weihenmayer, the blind climber who has summitted Everest and Denali, has an interesting perspective on climbing. "There's nothing to a summit. It's all in your mind. You don't suffer on a mountain for a month for just the view; it's the process. You feel your muscles getting you there, the weight on your back, the wind in your face."

Of course, he was talking about hard-core climbing; the majority of our summits were relatively modest achievements. But the point holds. Highpointing is nearly as much about travel as it is about high places.

One of the great appeals of writing this book was simply visiting all fifty states. Before this project began, both of us had traveled a lot in the U.S.—bike trips, kayak trips, car trips—but we had gaping holes on our geographical résumés. Nels had hitchhiked from Seattle to the top of Alaska, but he'd never been to "Big Sky" Montana. I'd somehow managed to avoid Alaska—despite having read a dozen books about it—as well as significant chunks of the South and Midwest.

Fifteen highpoints or so into it, we hit a logjam. The number-one issue couples argue about is money, and while Nels and I might not have been a couple in the classic sense, this issue was driving us toward divorce. Somewhere between California and Oklahoma we experienced what *People* magazine would call "irreconcilable differences."

For a year we put the project on hold. While time and money were the main culprits, the reality was that climbing all fifty highpoints was a far bigger commitment than either of us had imagined. Invariably, though, once enough time passed we'd start to miss the mountains and ridiculous banter that consumed 68.8% of our time on the road. So we'd get back out there again. Twenty-something highpoints into it, we'd climbed all the "cool" mountains and had to face the puny highpoints down South and in the Midwest, most of which lacked the glamour that compelled us to do the book in the first place. When we finished those—and they took a while—there was that 20,320-foot monster at latitude 62 that we were drawn to and scared of. Climbing Denali was more formidable than five back-to-back climbs up Mt. Rainier.

But we did it—all except the last 300 feet of Gannett Peak in Wyoming and, for Nels, the last 5,000 feet of Denali. Which raises an interesting question: How important is the summit, anyway? It is and it isn't. That's the best answer we've come up with, and we've discussed it a lot. Denali is so much more than its summit—but it was important to me to continue until I was able to go no higher. Nels now wishes he had made it to the top—for no other reason than he missed the opportunity to take some incredible photographs. He may well try again, just as we've made plans to revisit Gannett together.

Climbing state highpoints is like taking on a massive mountain. It's not the fifty summits that make the project worthwhile, it's the supreme satisfaction of committing to an ambitious, wild idea and then making it happen, however long it takes and whatever barriers—physical and emotional—you encounter. It doesn't matter how far you get, as long as you get as far as you can.

—J.G.
—N.A.

ACKNOWLEDGMENTS

DURING THE FIVE YEARS that it took us to complete this book, Nels and I were fortunate to receive assistance from a bunch of fine people. Mountain Hardware gave us lots of great gear. The MH logo saw its way to the top of every sizeable mountain we climbed. We're also grateful that just prior to heading to Alaska, we hooked up with Derek Doucet at Climb High Inc. in Shelburne, Vermont. I, at least, had the decency to change my next-to-skin Mammut expedition underwear two weeks up Denali; Nels did not. At the airport in Talkeetna, a Spanish climber begged me to trade my baseball cap with Mammut's Wooly Mammoth logo. I refused. It remains a cherished memento from the climb.

We'd also like to thank Maury McKinley at the International Mountain Climbing School (IMCS), for his expertise on Mt. Washington and sage advice about climbing Denali. We were fortunate to climb with some other terrific guides as well: the unflappable Ryan Hokenson; Kirby "Curbside" Spangler, who taught me more about self-arrest than any guy in Brooklyn needs to know (three years after we climbed with Kirby on Mt. Hood, we bumped into him at 15,000 feet on Denali), and RMI guides Kurt Wedberg and Matt Hartman, who helped make our five-day climb on Mt. Rainier seamless. We especially want to acknowledge Chris Hooyman, the third guide on our Rainier trip, who died on Denali the following summer helping a client. Chris was selfless, vibrant, and immensely likeable, and his death is a terrible loss. We were also privileged to climb with Vern Tejas, the best high-altitude mountain guide in the world. His calm, good cheer and shocking singing made that sublime and scary mountain far more hospitable. Spend three weeks with Tejas at altitude and you begin to see what inner strength is all about. John Colver, his stand-up co-guide, carved a mean ice sculpture. And many thanks to Gordon Janow at Alpine Ascents International. Before heading to Alaska, I called Gordon approximately 108 times. After a while he wised up and stopped taking my calls. (Prior to that he was quite helpful.) In fact, Gordon is a writer's best friend.

We also want to sincerely thank our editor Barbara Harold. No matter how many delays we encountered—and there were more than a few—she remained supportive and relentlessly positive. Jack Longacre, the caretaker of Taum Sauk in Missouri, escorted us to the highpoint and was gracious enough to write the Foreword—thanks, Jack. Anna Brahmstedt deserves special mention for enduring Nels' constant harassment via cell phone during all our time on the road and helping with our endless travel arrangements.

And finally, I owe a huge debt of gratitude to my wife, Beth Umland. Without her love and support it's unlikely I'd have made it through such a demanding project. Much of what is amusing and literate in this book comes as a result of her wise council, intellect, and sharp pencil. Only Beth and I know how much she did to improve the text.

INDEX

INDEX continued